Preserving
Positivity

Choosing to stay in the classroom and banishing a negative mindset

Haili Hughes

First published 2020

by John Catt Educational Ltd,
15 Riduna Park, Station Road,
Melton, Woodbridge IP12 1QT

Tel: +44 (0) 1394 389850
Fax: +44 (0) 1394 386893
Email: enquiries@johncatt.com
Website: www.johncatt.com

ISBN: 978 1 913622 00 8

Set and designed by John Catt Educational Limited

Testimonials

This brilliant book clearly and cleverly unpicks the problems that sit at the heart of the teacher retention crisis in our schools. As well as setting out what has gone wrong, Haili Hughes points to what teachers can do to seize back control of the profession and with it their lives. This may be the most important book on the state of teaching I have read and I would urge every teacher and school leader to read and reflect on these points as a matter of urgency.

Mark Enser, head of geography and research lead,
author of *Teach Like Nobody's Watching* and TES columnist

I watched from the Twitter sidelines as this book was imagined, conceptualised, debated and crowd-sourced, with Haili engaging with teachers and school leaders to explore their stories and her own. With 'Positivity' in its title, the book could have presented teaching through rose-tinted glasses – those heart-warming moments and pride in others' achievements that drip like treacle from some authors. Instead, Haili has asked why teachers leave, and their narratives reveal achingly difficult situations some find themselves in. But the teachers' accounts are framed in an investigative lens, an analysis of trends and a critical discussion of the tensions inherent in contemporary teaching in the UK. This acknowledgement of reality creates the space for problem-solving. Individually and collectively, it is possible to improve teacher retention, and this book offers genuinely useful insights that we can all learn from.

Professor Rachel Lofthouse, Professor of Teacher Education
at Leeds Beckett and Director of CollectivEd

In the opening of this excellent book, Haili Hughes rightly highlights that experienced teachers are 'the stalwarts of a school'. How refreshing to read a book that focuses on these individuals: that committed group who have devoted a career to teaching, but may find themselves dissatisfied with extensive demands on them. *Preserving Positivity* takes a captivating approach to inspiring and helping these teachers, interweaving Haili's own diverse experience in the profession with the voices of a huge range of teachers and leaders. Yes, it exposes some serious flaws with how our system is treating teachers, but it never loses the optimism and pragmatism that shines through it. This is a book that provides deeply practical strategies for each of the retention challenges, and will have a real impact in improving how teachers function and support each other. Individual ownership is so important in thriving as a teacher, and this important book teaches us that we need to take proactive and disciplined steps to managing the demands on us. It shines a deserved light on those "stalwarts", and will encourage so many of them to persevere with a challenging but wonderful profession.

Jamie Thom, English teacher and author,
host of *The Well Teacher* podcast

This book is a forensic, warts-and-all analysis of the realities of teaching. Hughes doesn't shy away from the darker aspects of the profession, but manages to present the truth with undimmed positivity and pragmatism. Enhanced by compelling accounts from real working teachers, this book cries out for change, understanding and, most important of all, hope. We must do more to frame teaching as the wonderful career it is. Hughes is a powerful advocate for resilience and joy in the classroom.

Jennifer Webb, teacher, senior leader, author, speaker

Preserving Positivity is an eye-opening read for all those working in the education sector. In the midst of a recruitment and retention crisis, there is a genuine need to explore the reasons teachers are citing for leaving the profession. Drawing on a range of lived experiences from education professionals, Haili Hughes offers her readers an insight into the challenges practitioners are facing, whilst also offering a range of practical solutions which may contribute towards tackling these very real issues in education.

Sarah Mullin, deputy head teacher, EdD student

In *Preserving Positivity*, Haili Hughes reveals contemporary education in England to be both the best of times and the worst of times. This perceptive account of the challenges faced by teachers offers a compelling personal story, alongside a wealth of experienced teacher voices that all share their experiences and insights with honesty. Hughes takes on the several issues and challenges faced by teachers today with honesty, but ultimately this book is fuelled by hope. It is well worth a read to reflect upon your school experiences and to recharge yourself with positivity.

Alex Quigley, National Content Manager at the
Education Endowment Foundation, former English teacher,
author of *Closing the Reading Gap*

This book is dedicated to my family, who supported my journey into the classroom, and to my husband, whose constant support has helped me to stay there.

Contents

Foreword

It is a privilege to write the foreword to a book written by someone who is so genuinely passionate about teaching that she is unafraid to be totally honest about the challenges facing the profession. Teacher recruitment and retention have never been more of a priority. The new Early Years Framework is testament to this, and the statistics must concern us all. Haili Hughes confronts in turn each of the known issues that people have cited as reasons for leaving their jobs. She provides personal stories for readers to reflect on as well as practical strategies for ways to overcome these challenges. Haili can be trusted, as she is so honest. Her love of teaching, young people and the full school community are the drivers for her writing this book. By helping others manage the doubts and perfectionism that seem to affect so many of our best teachers, she hopes that these teachers can stay in the job she loves.

The value of experienced and resilient staff in the staffroom, the value of having boundaries and knowing when good enough is good enough, and the importance of working in a school whose values you share are all evidenced by extensive research as well as personal experience. This isn't just a book for staff considering leaving teaching, but a celebration of why people stay and why we each need to consider our role in reducing burdensome assessment practices, inflexible thinking and work schedules, and value colleagues as people with full and rich lives outside of school.

Educating young people is hugely important to every society, and we need teachers who feel energised, purposeful, skilful and motivated. We need staff who feel that their needs are met and that they receive recognition and support for the challenging job they do. Many staff at all levels give so generously of their time and energy, but if staff are to stay for the long term, this needs to be consciously and thoughtfully managed. This book makes a real contribution to the debate on how to achieve this magical balance, which will be different for each one of us, and provides practical support to help achieve it.

Patsy Kane MA OBE
Mother of two, thirty-eight years working in schools

List of acronyms

ASCL   Association of School and College Leaders
AST   Advanced Skills Teacher
BAME Black, Asian and Minority Ethnic
CBT   Cognitive Behaviour Therapy
CPD   Continuing Professional Development
DfE   Department for Education
FE   Further Education
HMI   Her Majesty's Inspector
HoD   Head of Department
HSE   Health and Safety Executive
INSET In-School Training
IPS   Integrated Primary School
JCQ   Joint Council for Qualifications
LEA   Local Education Authority
LGBTQ Lesbian, Gay, Bisexual, Transgender and Questioning
LP   Lead Practitioner
MFL   Modern Foreign Languages
NPQML National Professional Qualification for Middle Leadership
NQT   Newly Qualified Teacher
Ofqual Office of Qualifications and Examinations Regulation
Ofsted Office for Standards in Education, Children's Services and Skills
PGCE Postgraduate Certificate in Education
PPA   Planning, Preparation and Assessment
PRP   Performance-Related Pay
PRU   Pupil Referral Unit

PSHE   Personal, Social, Health and Economic Education
RIBA   Royal Institute of British Architects
RQT   Recently Qualified Teacher
SAT   Standard Attainment Test
SEMH   Social, Emotional and Mental Health
SEN   Special Educational Needs
SENCo Special Educational Needs Coordinator
SEND   Special Educational Needs and Disability
SKE   Subject Knowledge Enhancement
SLD   Severe Learning Difficulties
SLE   Specialist Leader of Education
SLT   Senior Leadership Team
SOW   Scheme of Work
TLR   Teaching and Learning Responsibility
UPS   Upper Pay Scale
YA   Young Adult

Introduction

'The only source of knowledge is experience.' — Albert Einstein

Experienced teachers are the backbone of any school. Their skills and tried and tested methods provide a quality first education for their students. They have been around the block – seeing 'new' initiatives come around again and again – and, because of years spent navigating the shifting sands of policy transformation in education, they are calm in the face of change. They've met every type of pupil, so know how to deal with behaviour issues and placate parents on parents' evening. Their subject knowledge is honed by years of research, so they are confident to take risks and embrace new strategies. They have weapons in their arsenal, and they have fought a war rather than a battle. So why are they so undervalued?

Now, more than ever, experienced classroom teachers are feeling abandoned. We have all seen the headlines about the current recruitment and retention crisis, which is reportedly the worst for nearly 40 years (the *Daily Mirror*, 2019). But most of the retention strategies put in place by the Department for Education (DfE) seem to centre around the early career teacher: incentives for recruiting and retaining new and early career teachers seem to abound. These include higher rates of pay, golden hellos and even bursaries to pay for courses or living costs while the trainee teacher is studying.

However, these cash incentives don't seem to be working. They are an initial draw for people to enter the profession, but just don't seem to be keeping them there, with one in three teachers still leaving the profession before they have served five years in the classroom (the *Guardian*, 2019b). While all of this has been going on, experienced teachers have been struggling quietly in the background, with little support and encouragement or opportunities. Therefore, it's no surprise that there are hugely worrying signs in the teacher labour market. Some research from the Policy Exchange (2016) found that teaching does not follow a predictable linear pattern; from the 50,000 entrants into state teaching every year, roughly a third of these are experienced teachers returning to the profession. Therefore, much of the work that the DfE is doing in thinking up incentives that focus on attracting new people to the profession is somewhat missing the point.

Of course, recruiting newly qualified teachers is important, but keeping hold of experienced teachers, who are the stalwarts of a school, is just as vital. At a recent Women Leading in Education conference, Head of Technology at Sky, Louise Elliott, talked about the importance of having people who have been through tough times in education to be there as an example of resilience: 'people who've had those hard knocks', who can advise those new to the profession and benefit them with their wisdom and expertise. I found myself nodding away during her speech, remembering the staffroom of my early career, which was filled with wise old sages. Where have they all gone? Countless times as an early career teacher, I retired to the staffroom at break and lunch, with my tail between my legs after a particularly tough lesson, only to be encouraged and buoyed by my more experienced colleagues. Now many people spend their lunches in their classrooms answering emails or cramming in the other admin that they simply do not have time for in their school day.

It is certainly not only new teachers who feel unable to carry on in teaching. According to the Education Policy Institute (2018), exit rates have increased since 2010 to around 8 to 9 per cent in primary schools and 9.5 to 10.5 per cent in secondary schools. Concerningly, around 80 per cent of exits from the profession have been due to teachers pursuing other careers outside of the state-funded sector. Welcome to England's classrooms. Stories of experienced teachers who have left the profession for industry, retired early and taken a financial hit, or had a breakdown and been signed off work with stress are all too common. From my own personal experiences in school over the last 13 years, I have seen exceptional colleagues chewed up and spat out by the system, and the people who suffer the most are the students. I was someone who struggled with the system myself.

In 2008, after doing a few placements at secondary schools in Warrington, I decided to change careers, having been a national newspaper journalist in London. I can't say I had some deep-seated desire to teach. I had always wanted to be a journalist, but after a few years working at an infamous tabloid newspaper, my morals and self-worth couldn't cope with the increasingly bizarre things I was being asked to do in pursuit of an exclusive story. I wondered what else I could do with an English degree and made the decision to try out teaching. A few weeks into my first placement and I was hooked. After my Postgraduate Certificate in Education (PGCE), I joined my dream school with an incredibly experienced and supportive head of department, who saw my worth and value straight away. I was very quickly promoted into a middle leader position and, rather naïvely I think now, I wanted to go all of the way to headship. As a naturally ambitious person, this seemed like the only obvious progression to me and I thought it would all be easy.

However, things started to go wrong. The school got a disastrous set of GCSE results and dropped over 40 per cent in their headline measures for English and maths. Ofsted (the Office for Standards in Education, Children's Services and Skills) swooped in and judged the school as 'Special Measures' and the amazing curriculum leader I had learned so much from crumpled under the pressure. Unable to handle the criticism and finger pointing, where just a week before there had been praise, she left at the end of the week we got the judgement and never returned. Only four years into my teaching career, I found myself being catapulted into her role. Head of English in a school in a category, with no second in department and a staff member on long-term sick leave, I was horrendously out of my depth. Days were spent setting cover and marking hundreds of pieces of controlled assessments for three year 11 classes I was forced to take on. The behaviour at the school was poor, so often supply teachers would arrive in the morning and abandon the class by break, meaning I sometimes had to teach two classes at once, leaving the doors open and popping from room to room to check progress between tasks. I had a brilliant team, but they were all buckling under the pressure too.

My evenings were also not my own. Foolishly, I had synced my work emails to my mobile phone so that I had no nasty surprises when I logged on in the mornings. Members of the SLT (Senior Leadership Team) would regularly send emails late into the evening, demanding data tasks be completed by 9 a.m. the next morning, meaning I had to get out of bed to complete the task, as I knew I wouldn't have time in the morning because of setting cover and other duties. I was on the verge of a breakdown and something had to give. One night, in desperation, I broke down to my husband and told him that I couldn't carry on any longer. He told me to strip it all back and think about what had made me join the profession in the first place: the kids. I felt like my teaching was suffering and I wanted to get back to the classroom, step back from leadership and focus on developing my craft and my pedagogy. I wanted to become the 'Outstanding' teacher I had set out to be and I couldn't do that while I was trapped at my desk, filling in paperwork or crunching data and firefighting staffing problems.

So I stupidly/bravely resigned. I stepped down from the position I had worked so hard to achieve – my first rung on the ladder to headship – and went back to being 'just' a classroom teacher. Not only did it save my sanity, but it saved my career. Once again, I enjoyed coming into work. I experienced the immense satisfaction of knowing that I was a great teacher, that I was inspiring the next generation to love English, and that I could also go home and spend time with my own family without feeling a sense of guilt. This change of school and role was make or break for me; I would either begin to enjoy my job again, or, like many before me, I would leave the profession. With a new school, some research on coping strategies, and support from my peers at school and on Twitter, I have regained my love and passion for teaching. I once again feel that I can do this for the rest of my working life and that, although I still have difficult days, the good outweighs the bad in this incredible job.

I feel immense privilege to be a teacher. Now I want to help other teachers feel the same (which is how this book began to be realised) by empowering them with the skills and advice to feel a sense of positivity about staying in the classroom long term. I want to show them that there is an alternative to feeling forced into seeking a management position, as it isn't the only way to feel fulfilled or gain new experiences. I want to stop amazing, experienced teachers leaving the profession and enable them to realise that their unique experiences make them invaluable to our children. Bringing together existing up-to-date research and wisdom from those in the profession, *Preserving Positivity* will equip experienced teachers with some strategies and ideas to re-invigorate their practice and support them to remember that they are truly privileged to do the best job in the world.

Each chapter takes the theme of one of the reasons that teachers frequently cite for wanting to leave the profession in the Department for Education research report 'Factors affecting teacher retention: qualitative investigation' (2018) and starts with a literature review of the current research around the problem, exploring the context of why it's a significant factor. This factor will then be linked to my personal perspective and experiences as a classroom teacher of over a decade, drawing also on the wisdom of other teachers, through new qualitative research exclusively conducted for this book – the voices of the profession. In presenting these voices, I have endeavoured to preserve their authenticity, so only minor changes have been made for editorial purposes. The chapters then conclude with some takeaway tips and practical strategies entitled 'What can I do?', so that you have tangible strategies and ideas to try in your own classrooms. I want experienced classroom teachers to no longer have to feel alone and to remember that they are especially valued and supported.

I know how you may be feeling. I have been there. But I believe that there is another way and you do not need to leave the classroom to find happiness and balance. After all, education would be much poorer without you.

Chapter 1
Reason to leave #1: Work-life balance
How to make having a family and teaching work

The context

Many men and women work full-time jobs and manage to successfully raise families, somehow finding the balance between working to live and living to work. But what is it about teaching that makes this so difficult to manage? The public's perception of a teacher's working day certainly doesn't help. I can't count the number of humorous comments I have had about working half days and all of those holidays, but the truth about teachers' working hours is far from laughable. Teachers from the UK work an average of eight hours longer than their counterparts in other European countries, Australia and the United States. In fact, one in four teachers works in excess of 60 hours per week and almost half work most evenings (University College London, 2019). According to the DfE's Teacher Workload Survey in 2019 (DfE, 2019c), teachers in secondary schools reported working an average of 49.5 hours a week, while primary colleagues reported working 50 hours. While this is less than was reported in the 2016 Teacher Workload Survey, it is still over ten hours more than an average working week in industry in the UK.

Figure 1: Average working hours of full-time teachers and middle leaders during the reference week by phase (Source: DfE Teacher Workload Survey, 2019c)

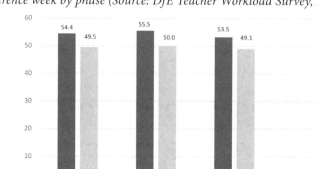

However, it isn't just the physical workload such as the marking, planning and paperwork that makes teaching an around-the-clock profession. It's the emotional strain as well. I'm sure many of us have been in the position where we can't sleep at night because of something we saw or overheard that day, or have felt sick at the scrutiny we are under with data analysis and progress measures. Mary Bousted, general secretary of the National Education Union, told the *Guardian* newspaper (2018b) that:

> There's a toxic mix of factors, created by this government, that is making teachers decide they cannot teach anymore. There is systemic overworking, with teachers routinely working 55 hours a week, and a vicious accountability system, which means teachers are not given the time and support to get better at what they do.

Just as worrying as the number of teachers leaving the profession are the 59 per cent of pre-retirement, serving teachers who are considering leaving in the next two years (Pearson, 2017). Around 6000 are women who are aged from 30 to 39 (DfE, 2014). The DfE, which conducted this survey, has used the term 'wastage' to describe teachers who have left the profession and are no longer in the classroom, and I have to agree. It is an incredible waste of their talents, experience and passion. It seems like no coincidence that this is also the prime age for women to have a family. It really is a tragedy that in the 21st century some women are still having to make a choice between having a successful teaching career and raising a family.

It seems the DfE has been making efforts to reduce teachers' workload and make teaching a more viable profession for those with a family. They have commissioned review groups to explore marking, data management, and planning and teaching resources. In addition, an advisory group was set up to research how best to stop the over reliance on data and evidence collection in schools, and the government accepted the recommendations made in the 2019 report, later writing a letter to urge local education authorities (LEAs) to stop the data burden on schools. In addition, the Education Secretary, Dominic Hinds, has produced a toolkit for school leaders and a handbook for governors to support them in being able to offer their staff a better work–life balance.

One way of achieving a better balance between home and work life is to encourage more flexibility in working hours. The DfE also commissioned some research into schools offering more flexible working for teachers, which resulted in a literature review, 'Exploring flexible working practice in schools', published in January 2019. The review aims to 'explore existing use of flexible practices in schools, and how flexible roles can be effectively designed and implemented in the sector', thus encouraging more schools to embrace part-time or flexible teachers (DfE, 2019a: 4). When teachers ask for more flexibility in their working hours, this is not an indication that they are not dedicated to their work or not as interested in their own continuing professional development (CPD) as are full-time teachers; they just wish to achieve a better balance between caring for a family and enjoying a fulfilling career. So, with the DfE seeming to understand the problem with achieving a work–life balance for teachers with families, why are so many head teachers still reluctant to offer more flexible working options for parents?

Unfortunately, for some teachers, even returning to work after maternity leave can be overwhelming. Whilst maternity leave is of course a time for recovery, bonding with a new baby and generally establishing parenting roles and enjoying time with a new child, the simple act of having time away can make it difficult to return. Of course, any sort of transition has challenges, and the change to and from working to not working – and back again – can cause much anxiety. This was a realisation that came to English teacher Emma Sheppard while she was on her own maternity leave in 2016. While absent from school, she had a personal desire to maintain her 'teacher identity' through CPD and lacked the support she needed while struggling from making the transition from 'teacher' to 'mother'. Emma soon realised that there wasn't really anything available to help her with these issues and decided to create 'The MaternityTeacher PaternityTeacher Project' (MTPTP) to support others like her who were struggling to maintain a teacher identity during their leave. The project began as a series of blogs, widened into a website and coffee mornings in London, and then became a national network and CPD provider. The MTPTP's core work is all about 'inspiring, empowering and connecting teachers choosing to complete CPD on parental leave', but Emma sees her work as a tiny cog in a much larger wheel of teacher retention and gender equity in educational leadership. Although there is little evidence to link maternity leave and the difficulties surrounding the transition back into work with the wastage of women aged 30 to 39 in teaching, it seems logical that this is a factor. Emma's theory is that by empowering teachers on maternity leave to complete CPD and retain their teacher identity if they so choose, and keeping them connected with a network of colleagues in the same situation, we are more likely to retain them following maternity leave and empower them to continue their career progression if they so choose. The project has been incredibly successful, building up a huge network on social media and formulating an accreditation programme, with more than 100 teachers receiving coaching as part of the Accreditation, Return to Work or Transition coaching programmes. She also provides a vital community for fathers and teachers who are now back at work, engaging with issues related to 'maternity leave' such as shared parental leave, provision for employees undertaking fertility treatment, finances associated with maternity leave, and general gender bias in the education system.

Figure 2: Links between gender and teacher retention (Source: The MaternityTeacher PaternityTeacher Project, 2019)

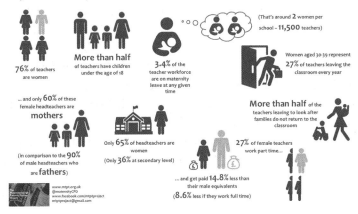

The success of the MTPTP has meant that many parents are now working flexibly successfully, but the benefits and success of flexible working arrangements are not just anecdotal. Many studies have recorded correlations between flexible working and better well-being (Almer & Kaplan, 2002; Gajendran & Harrison, 2007; Glass & Finley, 2002) and higher productivity and performance (Baltes, Briggs, Huff, Wright & Neuman, 1999; Bloom, Liang, Roberts & Ying, 2015; Perry-Smith & Blum, 2000).

Furthermore, returning to work and facing extortionate nursery or childcare costs are another reason that some teachers are finding it difficult to work full-time with a family. In the UK, the average cost of sending a child under two to nursery full-time is £242 per week (Family and Childcare Trust, 2018). Of course, millions of people across the UK must stump up this cash, so teaching is no different. However, many nurseries still ask for full payment during the holidays, so there is no flexibility for teachers who may want to take their child out and spend the holidays with them. While this can sometimes be a godsend if you have exam marking to do, it seems like a huge waste of over £1000 if you do take your child out for the whole of the six-week summer holiday.

To add to this, there is the huge hike in holiday prices at the times when teachers can plan a vital family holiday. A study showed that a holiday for two adults and two children costs on average over £900 more in August than the same holiday in July. Shockingly, holidays in August can cost as much as £3000 more than they do in June! (FairFX, 2017). It is no wonder, then, that some parents decide to risk a fine and take their children out of school so that they can book an off-peak holiday. Yet teachers do not have that luxury, as their holidays are set and they cannot have any time off outside of the school's set term dates. This can make it really difficult to have that family time to rest and recuperate that everybody needs. Nimish Lad wrote recently in the *TES* about their struggle as a teacher to plan a holiday abroad: 'In my 13 years of teaching, I've managed two holidays abroad that have lasted longer than a week; the rest have been four or five nights maximum. The cost has put us off going abroad three times already this year' (*TES*, 2019a).

What's more, so much of the holidays are taken up with the odd jobs and appointments that there is just no time for during term time that there is scant time for a break. Although my husband is not a teacher, he is in education and works to set term times too. We have regularly lived with many broken household items until we have space to breathe in the holidays and one of us gets the energy to fix them. Then there are the medical and dental visits, which you daren't have asked for time off for during the last term, or even catching up with the friends and family you haven't seen for months because of your back-to-back twelve-hour days. Even attempting to fit a holiday into this crazy schedule can be an achievement.

My story

I came into teaching as a new mother of a four-month-old baby boy, so I have never known anything other than trying to balance my career and family. I had quit my high-profile job in journalism while pregnant, thinking that teaching would be a much more family friendly career. Parenthood is a job that requires us to give up almost all of our time and energy for the well-being of another. Alas, so is teaching, and by their nature, many teachers will just keep giving until they have nothing left to give. This is the position I found myself in as an idealistic newly qualified teacher (NQT) – marking and planning meticulously until the small hours, while getting up five or six times a night with a new baby. But it seemed like a price I was willing to pay, because the sheer exhaustion and crazy working hours seemed to be paying off in the relationships I was building with the young people in my care. I felt an immense job satisfaction and told myself that things would get easier as I gained more experience and my son grew up.

But they didn't.

Nobody tells you that children need just as much of your time and energy – if not even more – as they grow up than they do when they are babies.

Dragging yourself out of bed, pouring with sweat from a fever, while ministering to your screaming baby who is also ill, just to set cover work at 6 a.m., seems like a situation that is quite unique to teaching. I am probably not alone in having dropped my child at nursery, dosed up with Calpol when they probably needed a day off at home with Mummy cuddles, as I knew that year 11 still had 8 more poems to study before their exam and we were running out of time. I have been guilty of choosing other people's children over my own so many times that it makes me quite sick with guilt to think about it.

That is not to mention the plays and assemblies and sports days…all missed because I didn't dare ask for cover. I tried for a second baby for 9 years and finally succeeded when my son was about to start year 6 in primary school. It was amazing to be able to attend all of his assemblies and events while I was on maternity leave. For the first time in his life, I was able to drop him off at school and pick him up, to hear on the walk home about what he had done during his day, and to speak to his teachers if needed. I felt like a real parent.

Now my son is in secondary school – the school I work at – so although he is too cool to walk in with me in the mornings, I do sometimes bump into him during the day. A few weeks ago, he was ill and a colleague from reception came upstairs to tell me while I was in the middle of teaching year 10. It was nice to be able to go down to him and hug him while he had a little cry. It made me think about all of the times he must have been upset at primary school and had nobody there to come and comfort him.

Yet high school has brought its challenges. After having boundless patience to cope with the mood swings of other people's teenagers, it can be difficult to come home at the end of a 12-hour day and face the attitude of your own! The homework is also proving to be a hard slog. Sometimes I feel that in the evenings I can barely face pushing him to complete his homework after pushing year 11 all day, but I kill myself getting my students through their exams, so I know that I have got to put in the same effort for my own child.

Like many experienced teachers, I have felt like a poor parent, constantly checking the clock to see if it is close to bedtime so I can turn my laptop back on or finish my marking. The worst are the evening CPD sessions, meetings and parents' evenings. I leave the house at 7 a.m. and don't see my children all day. When it is parents' evening, I don't even get to kiss them goodnight. Both roles in my life are all-consuming and I know I am not alone in these experiences.

Voices from the profession

Tamsen Jones, teacher of English

I'm a first-time mum of (now) four-year-old twins. While I like to think I was quite organised before they were born, their arrival really taught me the value of schedules. Before I had the children, I didn't worry too much about not getting everything done at school, as I could always switch on the laptop in front of the TV later, or catch up with marking in the evening, but once you have children, there may not be a 'later' to do your schoolwork at home. Everything has to be optimised to happen at school, during your working hours.

The first schedule I adopted was the Baby Whisperer's E.A.S.Y routine for the twins: Eat–Activity–Sleep–Your time.* To look at them, they don't

---

* The reference to this routine is not an endorsement by the author of *Preserving Positivity* of any particular routine or parenting style and does not suggest that one style is better than another.

seem like they would make life that much easier, but believe me, they really helped. It meant that my babies had a very clear routine, I knew why they were crying, and there was no mummy guilt, which can be the real killer. It also helped when I went back to work full-time and I was able to give that schedule to the nursery and grandparents who helped with childcare.

By the time I had the twins, I had been teaching ten years, and it's still a continuing process of tweaking routines.

Figure 3: Example of E.A.S.Y baby routine

E: Eat   A: Activity   S: Sleep   Y: You

3 Hour E.A.S.Y	4 Hour E.A.S.Y
E: 7:00 wake up and feed A: 7:30 or 7:45 depending how long feed takes S: 8:30 1.5hr nap Y: Your choice	E: 7:00 wake up and feed A: 7:30 S: 1.5hr nap Y: Your choice
E: 10:00 A: 10:30–10:45 S: 11:30 1.5hr nap Y: Your choice	E: 11:00 A: 11:30 S: 1.5–2hrs at 13:00 Y: Your choice
E: 13:00 A: 13:30 or 13:45 S: 14:30 1.5hr nap Y: Your choice	E: 15:00 A: 15:30 S: 17:00 or 18:00 or somewhere in between: catnap Y: Your choice
E: 16:00 feed S: 17:00 or 18:00 or somewhere in between: catnap for 40 minutes or somewhere in between to get baby through the next feed and bath	E: Cluster feed at 19:00 and 21:00 if going through growth spurt A: Bath S: 19:30 bedtime Y: The evening is yours!
E: Cluster feed at 19:00 and 21:00 if going through a growth spurt A: Bath S: 19:30 bedtime Y: The evening is yours!	E: Dream feed until 7 or 8 months or until solid food is firmly established
E: 22:00 or 23:00 dream feed	

After having the twins, I did think about going part-time, but was told that this wouldn't be possible. The official line was that the school didn't want to split classes, as that would be damaging to pupils' learning – which we know has been debunked – but fortunately I was able to extend my leave to a year, returned in January, and before the half term had a new position set for September. The school was definitely a toxic school, and the loss of three 'Outstanding' teachers as a result of its unwillingness to allow part-time work was just the start. The next year, many more left.

Having a routine has really helped me manage it, though, and I even go as far as creating a live marking schedule for my classes; I aim to check in with four pupils per lesson (more if it's a shorter piece of work) over a two-week period, so basically I've had a one-to-one conversation with each child at LEAST twice a half term. Teaching English can be a nightmare for marking, but by doing things like this I have significantly lowered my workload. I have also been using a lot of retrieval practice, so pupils self-mark a lot. This has helped me avoid drowning in my own good intentions and the expectations of others.

Of course, a lot of this depends on your school and department. It basically boils down to having well-planned schemes of work (SOWs) and an assessment plan that includes formative assessment and a feedback (not marking) policy. Another good tip is to create work booklets in advance! If your toddler has a meltdown, you don't want to deal with a photocopy machine meltdown and then your own subsequent meltdown at the same time!

Catherine Carden, faculty director of teaching and learning

In almost every study you look at, a lot of the people wanting to leave teaching point to a lack of work–life balance. The moves made by government have gone some way to reducing workload, but so far it is not making as huge an impact as it could do. I think a lot of this comes down to the fact that teachers are committed and selfless professionals. Seeing the children for whom they're responsible achieve is important to teachers; it's what they strive for. As a result, teachers are constantly looking to do things better – to deliver the perfect lesson, a great set of SAT (standard attainment test) outcomes, excellent behaviour, and a stunning set of exercise books showing significant progress. Teachers constantly aim to be 'Outstanding'.

I have found that the easiest way of beginning to find a work–life balance is to instead accept that a work–life balance is ultimately unattainable. After reading Joanna Barsh and Susie Cranston's advice in their book, *How Remarkable Women Lead: The breakthrough model for work and life*, I realised that it may be this desire for perfection and achieving that work–life balance that causes the stress and pressure teachers sometimes feel. They suggest that we stop aspiring to this unattainable ideal and instead seek to establish a 'managed disequilibrium'.

A managed disequilibrium is realistic, as it helps us to admit that there are going to be times when work takes precedence and will predominantly fill our lives, both in and outside of working hours. Sometimes, there will be late evening work and weekend marking, but we don't need to beat ourselves up, as sometimes this will tip the other way and work can be put on the back burner. That way, when there are fewer pressures from work, you can leave at the end of the school day and enjoy more time with your family at weekends.

In my opinion, for us to be able to cope with the demands of this all-encompassing job, we have to accept this disequilibrium and try to manage it – rather than striving for a consistent perfect work and family life balance that doesn't exist. It is all about managing and planning it by identifying and planning when the busy times will be, such as after mock exams, while also ring-fencing time for our personal lives at less busy times.

Ryn Jones, teacher of English

Being on maternity leave can feel like you are distanced from your department at the best of times. When things are going on around you, it's easy to feel like an outsider. But it can be even more difficult when even your own position changes in your absence. This happened to me each time I was on maternity leave, with the department getting a 'restructure'.

The first time this happened, I went from key stage 3 coordinator to 'data and assessment', and then on the second time I changed to 'intervention'. It became clear that they had asked the other coordinator what they wanted to do and then left me with everything else – without even discussing it with me.

It seemed to me that there was more to it, and after my second maternity leave, I was called into a surprise meeting with the deputy head and my HoD (head of department), who was given the job whilst I was on maternity leave, where they pulled me apart for 40 minutes, threatened me with removing my TLR (teaching and learning responsibility) and then sent me straight in to teach, crying my eyes out. I wasn't going to take this lying down, and I spent that lesson crafting a reasoned complaint, which outlined the fact that I knew that my rights had been breached.

They were clearly rattled, offering me support after this and leaving me alone. I stayed there until the end of that academic year and took an effective pay cut (through travel expenses) in order to get out. The advice I would give is to know your rights. I investigated maternity leave law and discovered that if we go on maternity leave before the February half term, we are owed holidays, for example, and I was never given that option. I won't let anyone be treated like that now that I'm in charge! I should probably have taken my grievance further, but I'm sad to say that I just left. By that time, I was pretty much broken in terms of self-esteem and I thought I was rubbish. Sixth months later, I was giving INSET (in-school training) to multiple schools on innovative teaching and was made HoD two years later. I now see that it wasn't me, and that knowing your rights is so important in fighting for that vital work–life balance.

Will Easton, semi-retired head teacher

I was moved to reflect on work–life balance following some chats with my dad and some reflective-thinking work I was doing with the National College.

My dad was a 'proper bloke' to his mates – a big man who fought in the war and worked with his hands until he was 65. There were no shades of grey with him: he worked; he came home; he provided; he went to the pub with his mates. He couldn't boil an egg and that never worried him. He did what society expected. Later in life, we became very good friends, but in my childhood, he was quite a distant character.

As I moved from college to teaching and later climbed the professional ladder, I found that I wasn't going to be like my dad and that expectations of me were quite different. There was a weight of expectation from myself and from society that I needed to be much more!

I was the typical eager young professional. Initially, my work–life balance was like my father's. I was living in the heady cultural mix of north London in the 1980s. I made friends, we went to the pub on Friday night, and we refereed football matches on Saturday mornings with horrendous hangovers. Later in the afternoon, we played football ourselves, running off the stresses of the week, and this inevitably led to more beer! But here is where my life veered away from my father's. We went back to our respective flats and houses and cooked from scratch for our partners, we washed, we cleaned, we did childcare and we entertained. We put huge pressure on the 'balance' aspect of our lives. It was no longer expected that we would just have a night down the pub with the boys; it had grown into this many-headed behemoth to be the perfect partner, perfect mate, perfect cook, perfect host. In some ways, Mondays were something of a relief, as it was then only a matter of being the perfect professional again. The upshot of trying to constantly please this behemoth was that we blew it...or in my case, my marriage ended. Then I had to totally reconstruct this balance.

In some ways, it became even more demanding, with a new partner, increased responsibility at work, being a godparent, balancing childcare and the hunger and desire to make each weekend or half term as full as possible for your children. But I didn't mind this. I almost enjoyed it.

Then the balance shifted again. In my case, my daughter became increasingly ill and no one could work out what it was, until eventually the blisters on her arms and face became too hard to dress at home and Alice spent three to four days a week in hospital, having dressings changed and her blood washed off every night. So now the 'balance' was all-consuming. It took over, because no child should suffer. By this time, I was a head teacher and working hard to improve young people's lives, except I couldn't improve Alice's; I could only drive and spend nights in a hospital chair as the doctors did their best. The weekends became hugely important and the free time became precious time together.

And then she died, and the demands of the balance were gone. There was work and there were the long evenings alone and the red, red wine and the long road to re-establish the balance, to ensure work didn't become all-consuming, because that's all the control I had. I needed to be there for the weekends and for my son, who in the wake of his sister's death had to carry on with his life. He moved in with me, but now he was 17, he had friends and his own life and he didn't need me to do the manual things, and so we grew a new balance in our life. He restarted his life; I restarted mine. We became increasingly aware that we were both quite fragile, and didn't quite know how to talk about it or deal with it, but we managed, and we established new work–life balances.

So we moved on, and now that I am partly retired, I can choose my work and am less stressed. The balance no longer has to be some highly structured aspect of my life. My son is now a special educational needs (SEN) teacher and stepping on the ladder, and he will work out his own work–life balance for himself. The best advice I can give to him and other teachers is that you never get over something like this, but you have to get on with it. Routine – often grinding routine – gives life structure. It would be easy to throw your hands up and disappear into a bottle, but that disrespects the life that has been lost.

Heidi Drake, teacher of English

When I had my first child back in 2015, my husband, a police officer, worked 9 to 5, but then joined a different team and changed to shift work. It was an odd pattern: three days; three lates; then three off. Except if the late was on a Friday or Saturday, it was actually a half night (5 p.m.–3 a.m.).

If I'm honest, this was quite lovely while I was on maternity leave. It meant we could do fun things like go away for the weekend on last-minute deals without using annual leave, and even when I returned to part-time work, we still managed to squeeze in a couple of 'Just for Tots' breaks. However, it became a lot more of an issue when I returned to work full-time.

For me personally, it became clear that to bring balance to my life I wanted to return full-time. This would enable me to take up a much bigger range of career development opportunities. We did the maths, and despite what we'd previously assumed, we could just about afford to put both the children in nursery full-time rather than just for three days a week. It wasn't until we were in the midst of being back at work that we thought about things like parents' evening and trying to balance my attendance at these with my husband's shift patterns. Somehow – I have no idea how – every single parents' evening fell on a late shift. Unfortunately, we don't have a large support network, so it has proved difficult to manage and arrange these, with lots of negotiations with both workplaces to find the best solution. Then it seemed like every school event also clashed with shift patterns; it was like they knew. If I had a pound for every sad-faced student when I said I couldn't come to the concert/play/rugby match, I wouldn't need to teach!

What I noticed even more, however, was the effect on my work–life balance. I couldn't do anything other than teach and parent. Being a teacher and being a parent is great, but everyone needs a place to be 'them'. I couldn't join a choir. I couldn't join any of the exercise groups I wanted to join. I couldn't even seem to manage to schedule a 'Couch to 5k'. The end result was, quite frankly, a rather grumpy and tired teacher and a sometimes strained relationship with the person who only ever seemed to be around for the nice things like holidays.

Now I know I am hugely privileged to have a partner and to be able to afford full-time nursery, but that doesn't mean that there aren't sacrifices. My children wake up by 5 a.m. every day, so my main sacrifice has been sleep. With everything like this you cope because you have to, but some simple steps have made things easier for us. Things such as using a family calendar on which to plot all shifts and school events makes planning much easier. This also means that planning in advance can have its advantages and children can be taken out of childcare to have memorable experiences with the shift worker. We did this with the Polar Express and it was amazing. I think it is also important to be open and honest and let your school leaders know if you are struggling. You don't have to say yes to everything – no can be a complete sentence.

What can I do?

The key tip from the hundreds of teachers I have spoken to is to accept help. Work together with your partner or extended support network so that everybody can share the load. Develop good relationships with colleagues who are in a similar situation, so you know that you are not alone. Teaching is just a career, but being a parent is so much more.

Many colleagues spoke about the importance of having clear routines and using some of the popular ready-made routines that are out there (some examples of these are included below). Another thing that really works for me is making lists – but don't overload them. Try to narrow things down to doing just a couple of things a day well and then you can cross them off as you go. It seems to me like I have really achieved something if I can cross an item from a list. But remember to prioritise. What you can't do can wait. Workable goals and intentions make things a habit rather than a chore.

A lot of the things that will help you achieve work–life balance are small tweaks that can be implemented at work. It starts with finding a school that is sympathetic to how difficult it is to raise a family and teach full-time. There are an increasing number of positions that are being advertised as job shares – even headships – and schools are becoming much more understanding about the need for staff to have a good balance. However, things that you can do yourself might be to use your PPA (planning, preparation and assessment) wisely. While it is tempting to sit and have a coffee with colleagues, instead why not seek out a room out of the way and spend the time doing some of the work you may have previously taken home with you? Another small change may be to create folders to file your emails into. It is common for me to receive as many as 150 emails a day and this can be incredibly overwhelming. Now I have my emails meticulously organised into folders and try to answer them as soon as I can, so that they don't build up and add to my stress levels.

Another quick tip is to do as much marking and feedback as you can while you are circulating the room during lessons. Get yourself a verbal feedback stamp and ask students to write a note of what your feedback was when you stamp their book. They can then check they acted on this feedback at the end of the lesson. If you need to mark a piece of work more thoroughly, ask pupils to open their books on the page the work is on and pile them up like this. This small action can cut at least half an hour off your marking, as it eliminates the time spent flicking through books looking for the work.

Outside of school, it is about drawing up our own boundaries and retraining our minds. We are conditioned through the perfect lives and portrayals of parenthood we see on our TVs and social media screens to believe that we need to strive for an impeccable ideal that just isn't possible. Yes, your house being clean and tidy creates less stress when you arrive home, but be realistic; it doesn't need to be spotless. Accepting that nothing will ever be perfect is key.

Also, things like ordering a grocery box for shopping every week has cut out the stressful supermarket visits and means that I don't really have to think about what I am cooking. It is important to make dedicated time for your family and stick to it, even if this is just something silly like having a chat about your day over the dinner table or doing the bedtime routine of bath, story and bed. Since I stopped syncing my email to my phone and made a rule to put all phones away at 8 p.m., I have spent quality time with my husband and gone to bed in a much calmer mood, with thoughts of school not swimming around my mind. That data or marking will wait. Draw your line in permanent marker when it comes to working hours and do not compromise. This takes an enormous amount of self-discipline, but it is worth it.

Another intervention that many other teachers said helped was practising mindfulness. In a 2014 study, researchers conducted a 3-week online self-training intervention with 246 employees who were struggling with energy levels during non-work time, impairing their work–life balance. The study aimed to reduce unwanted psychological preoccupation with work concerns and used mindfulness as a strategy for employees to find their ideal way to segment their working and personal lives. The participants in the study reported that they 'experienced significantly less strain-based work–family conflict and significantly more psychological detachment and satisfaction with work–life balance' (Michel, Bosch & Rexroth, 2014: 1). Trying some simple mindfulness techniques can be great for separating the two spheres of working and personal life and can help bring calmness and clarity to any turbulence you're experiencing at work. Figure 4 is a mindfulness resource that will give you a start, but there are also thousands of resources online that can move this practice forward if you find it helps. Overwhelmingly, the message I received from every teacher I interviewed was to stick to your guns and find your voice: don't let anyone tell you what is best for you and your family.

Figure 4: Steps to mindfulness

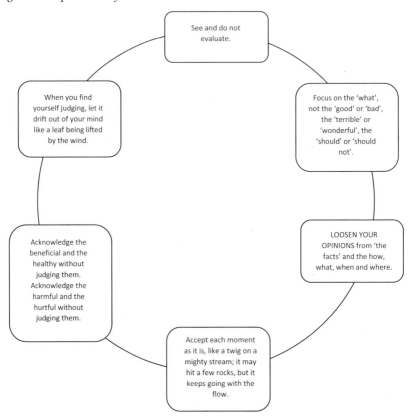

See and do not evaluate.

When you find yourself judging, let it drift out of your mind like a leaf being lifted by the wind.

Focus on the 'what', not the 'good' or 'bad', the 'terrible' or 'wonderful', the 'should' or 'should not'.

Acknowledge the beneficial and the healthy without judging them. Acknowledge the harmful and the hurtful without judging them.

LOOSEN YOUR OPINIONS from 'the facts' and the how, what, when and where.

Accept each moment as it is, like a twig on a mighty stream; it may hit a few rocks, but it keeps going with the flow.

5 *Useful* Mindfulness EXERCISES

MINDFUL HAND AWARENESS EXERCISE
Grasp your hands really tightly and hold for 5 to 10 seconds, then release and pay attention to how your hands feel. Keep your attention focused on the feeling for as long as you can.

MENTAL FOCUS EXERCISE
Stare at any object and try to remain focused on that object for as long as possible. Keep a mental watch on when your mind wants to wander and then just bring it back to the object. The longer you can remain focused, the more your mindfulness will increase.

MUSICAL STIMULI EXERCISE
Listen to your favourite song and pay attention to the way it makes you feel. What emotions does it stir? What memories come up and how do those memories make you feel? Engage the emotions and see where they lead.

UNDIVIDED ATTENTION EXERCISE
Do something around the house that you have never done before and do it with utter and undivided attention.

FULL SENSORY AWARENESS EXERCISE
Wherever you are, just stop and look around when safe to do so. Become aware of everything that your senses pick up. How do you feel? Do you feel overstimulated? Do you feel anxious? Make a metal note and keep on observing, without judgement.

Chapter 2
Reason to leave #2: Workload
A never-ending list...

The context

If you have been teaching for a while, chances are you will have heard some of these iconic comments from people not associated with the profession:

'You only work 8 to 4.'

'Part-timers'

'Imagine all those holidays.'

Obviously, the people making these comments must not have any connection with teachers or have ever worked in the classroom themselves. If they did, then they would realise that teaching is so much more than a job: it's an all-consuming vocation. Perhaps it is because of the holidays that teaching gets such a bad press – and they are very generous – but they are also badly needed. Until you too have lain awake at night, your mind buzzing with all of the work you have to complete, the worries you have about the child in your GCSE class who is crippled by anxiety and the 240 mock exam papers you somehow have to mark between teaching a full timetable and after-school intervention classes, you cannot begin to imagine the pressure and weight that being an educator carries with it. Unfortunately, the problem with teaching is that everybody has been to school, so they think they are experts on teachers' hours and workloads and have a right to comment on it. Yet more recently, as the COVID-19 virus has swept across the globe and governments have closed down schools to most children, my social media feeds are flooded with frustrated and frazzled parents who are realising the amazing jobs that teachers do and how much work they have to get through in a day. It seems that the public is now realising the immense role that teachers play in their students' lives, and the appreciation is great to hear.

The stats don't lie. Workload in teaching has been an issue affecting teacher retention for a long time. Research from Thomas et al. in 2004 found that teachers' working weeks were much more intensive than those of other professions (see Figure 5 below), and that despite teachers seemingly having so many holidays, a large proportion of these are used to complete work that they didn't manage to cram into the previous term or to undertake preparation for the next term. Of course, some may argue that when spread across a normal working year rather than an academic year the hours that teachers work are more evened out and in line with other professions. But this does not do justice to the sheer intensity of teaching. A good analogy is to be found in *Managing Teacher Workload*, where the authors write: 'As a job it has many similarities to acting, but no one would expect an actor to be on stage for five hours a day, five days a week and 39 weeks a year' (Bubb and Earley, 2004: 6).

However, although it is intense, the stuff in the classroom – the business of actually teaching – is not the problem. The problem is all of the extra things that just cannot be shoehorned into the school day. In the same survey, researchers found that around a quarter of teachers' work during term time took place outside of the standard UK working hours and that almost 20 per cent of that work took place after 6 p.m. or at weekends and before school started. It is difficult for those not in the profession to understand the sheer amount of bureaucracy and paperwork that floods teachers' working weeks. A recent survey by Teacher Tapp (2018) even found that reading emails alone can take up to six hours a week of an educator's time, which would be better spent on honing teaching and learning so that outcomes can be improved for students. In addition, the 2017–18 Labour Force Survey found that teaching was one of three professions with the highest reports of stress and depression, while 84 per cent of the 11,000 respondents to a survey by the teachers' union NASUWT in 2017 said workload was their number one concern.

Figure 5: Hours worked by teachers compared to other professions (Source: Thomas et al., University of Birmingham, 2003)

Occupation	Average weekly hours		Average total holiday hours		Total annual hours	
	STRB	UoB	PWC	UoB	STRB/PWC	UoB
	2000	2002	2001	2002		2002
Primary schools						
Head teachers	58.9	57.6	122.4	139.4	2,420	2,386
Deputy heads (1)	56.2	56.8	115.5	137.1	2,307	2,352
Classroom teachers	52.8	53.9	97.4	114.0	2,157	2,216
Secondary schools						
Head teachers	60.8	58.8	155.5	163.7	2,527	2,457
Deputy heads (1)	58.6	55.9	149.6	138.0	2,435	2,318
Heads of faculty (2)	52.9	51.7	149.6	121.1	2,213	2,137
Classroom teachers (3)	51.3	50.8	113.0	110.5	2,114	2,092
Special schools						
Classroom Teachers (2)	51.2	52.8	130.8	126.0	2,128	2,185
National averages for other managers and professionals						
All managers (ONS)	46.3		0		2,222	
All professionals (ONS)	44.0		0		2,112	

Notes:

(1) All leadership group except head teacher (deputy, assistant head, leadership group)
(2) All other teachers, excluding trainees
(3) Management points, recruitment and retention points, advanced skills teachers
(4) NQTs, main scale, upper scale

ONS – Office of National Statistics

Almost 20 years on from this initial research, not much has really changed...except more accountability for results, more stringent performance management and even more work piled onto teachers. In 2019, the *i* newspaper invited three teachers to keep a diary of their working day, and the results showed just how hectic and stressful teaching can be. The primary school teacher featured in the article started her working day at 7:30 a.m. and finished way after 6 p.m. – a far cry from the stereotypical 8 until 4 impression that many people have of a teacher's working day. The secondary school teacher spent until 10 p.m. marking work and planning lessons for his teaching the next day. These long hours cannot be conducive to well-being. Research suggests that the more manageable teachers feel their workloads are, the more job satisfaction they have (Lynch et al., 2016; Sims, 2017) and whether somebody is happy and satisfied in their job is closely linked to teacher retention (Bamford and Worth, 2017). Therefore, it is no wonder that workload is such a huge deciding factor when people choose to leave the profession.

Another large contributor to workload is all of the support and management activities that teachers spend time on, such as 'organising resources and premises, setting up displays and setting up/tidying classrooms'. The Teacher Workload Survey (DfE, 2019c) reported that secondary school teachers spent on average almost three hours a week doing this, while primary colleagues spent over three. However, the greatest amount of administrative time was spent on 'planning, administering and reporting on pupil assessments' (3.1 hours for primary; 2.7 hours for secondary) and 'recording, inputting, monitoring and analysing data in relation to pupil performance' (2.3 hours for primary; 2.0 hours for secondary). Teachers and middle leaders also reported spending 1.4 hours on 'school policy development and financial planning' in both phases. It is in this environment of high workload that teachers' psychological health suffers and they start to feel the symptoms of burnout. It is no surprise when examining these statistics that research across countries indicates that teachers report the highest levels of stress and burnout when compared with other contact professions (Heus & Diekstra, 1999; Schaufeli & Enzmann, 1998).

It is not just the physical exhaustion of long hours; it is the sheer emotional exhaustion that teachers suffer as they are often unable to just switch off like many other professions, but find themselves lying in bed thinking about the pressure they are under. Research has suggested that burnout is positively related to the intention to leave the teaching profession (Leung & Lee, 2006; Skaalvik & Skaalvik, 2011), so it's no surprise that teachers who report more emotional exhaustion will retire or leave the profession earlier. It is this kind of stress and pressure that is forcing teachers out of the profession in droves every year and has led to the retention problem we are currently suffering in the UK. But it has also led to recruitment issues, as graduates see that teaching can sometimes be an untenable career choice and are put off applying by the constant negative headlines. McGrath-Champ, Wilson, Stacey & Fitzgerald (2018) talk about how the increasing demand of the administrative tasks mentioned above are creating a 'blanketing' effect across schools which 'severely threaten[s] to overwhelm teachers' professional focus on teaching and student learning' (McGrath-Champ et al., 2018: 2). The uncontrollable beast that workload has become seems to be attacking the profession, and it is time that teachers fought back.

Perhaps the biggest pressure on teacher workload highlighted in the Teacher Workload Review in 2016, but not yet addressed in over 50 per cent of schools, is the unrealistic expectations associated with marking and feedback. Even Ofsted recognised that the way marking was scrutinised and reported on in previous inspection frameworks was simply making the expectations put on teachers even more unmanageable. After separate research from both the DfE and the Education Endowment Foundation in 2016, it became clear that there is little research evidence to prove that detailed and extensive marking has any significant impact on pupils' learning. This led to the National Director of Education, Sean Harford, telling inspectors to 'not report on marking practice, or make judgements on it, other than whether it follows the school's assessment policy' (Edison Learning, 2017). 'Eliminating unnecessary workload around marking: Report of the Independent Teacher Workload Review Group' (DfE, 2016) gave a clear message to school leaders and the expectations they were putting on their staff: 'If your current approach is unmanageable or disproportionate, stop it and adopt an approach that considers exactly what the marking needs to achieve for pupils.'

Unfortunately, in some schools, changing the marking policy is not even going to scrape the surface; working in a more challenging school, for example – a school which may have been placed in an Ofsted category 'Requires Improvement' or 'Inadequate' – can ramp up workload and pressures on staff even further. On average, teachers in these schools spent 0.7 more hours on 'individual planning and preparation of lessons' and 0.7 more hours on 'marking/correcting of pupils' work' compared to teachers and middle leaders in Ofsted category 'Good' schools (DfE, 2019c). This statistic resonates with me especially, as I have been in that position and I still bear the emotional scars.

My story

As a late entrant to the teaching profession who had already had a successful career in a high-pressured environment before I retrained, I really didn't think that the workload from teaching would cause me any problems. In my former life as a national newspaper journalist, I was constantly on call. News doesn't wait, and I could be asked to come to work in the middle of the night. To be honest, before I started teaching, like many members of the public I believed the dogma that teachers had all of those holidays and that it was a great career for people with families.

I started my PGCE when my son was just a few months old. I didn't drive and studied about 15 miles away, meaning I had to get the bus to university and to my placement schools. The lack of sleep with a newborn and the 5 a.m. starts meant I was often lulled to sleep on the warm bus journeys, uncomfortably jolted awake as I arrived – sometimes just in the nick of time! It wasn't easy or ideal, but we made it work. Luckily, my husband was very supportive, and Friday nights became my filing time, where we would open a bottle of red wine, lay all of my paperwork from that week on the living room floor, and file it away in my teaching standard evidence files.

In 2009, I landed the job of my dreams at a local school where I had done a placement for a couple of weeks and had fallen in love with the staff and kids. The school hadn't done as well as it could academically, but it was located in a very socially deprived area and the pastoral support was outstanding. Under the old framework, the school was judged as 'Satisfactory', and for my first few years there, they seemed quite happy to continue with what they were doing. The experiences and opportunities the pupils were given at this school were exemplary and results were going up, so it was definitely moving in the right direction.

From being an NQT, I rose quite quickly through the ranks. Perhaps it was my former experience of being in the workplace that made me a little less 'wet behind the ears' than other NQTs, but I also felt incredibly ambitious to progress. Within a couple of years, I was a middle leader and the department was very successful and going from strength to strength. In 2013, we celebrated achieving above the national average for the first time with our GCSE results. The head of English was superb – a really experienced and measured leader from whom I enjoyed learning. But the educational landscape was changing rapidly. Controlled assessment was disappearing, and speaking and listening grades, which had always helped our cohort achieve, were being downgraded. We didn't really make contingencies for this and our results plummeted, catapulting the school into 'Special Measures'. The curriculum leader went home that week and never came back, leaving me to pick up the pieces and try somehow to keep the department going.

For those who have never experienced being placed in a category, you probably have no conception of just how bad it is. 'Relentless' doesn't cover it. I already had 2 year 11 classes, but because of staff absence, I now had to take on an extra GCSE class. Behaviour was so bad at the school that supply teachers would either not turn up or leave early into a lesson. But the worst was the scrutiny: the regular visits from LEA advisors and special leaders of education (SLEs) from other schools, who tore apart our SOWs; the meetings where every little bit of data was pored over, and the midnight emails demanding that things be done before 9 a.m. the next morning. The cracks in my physical and mental well-being were being papered over, but it wasn't long before they began to show, and I am not ashamed to admit that I had a breakdown. I had two choices: one, leave the school, step down and try to rediscover my love for teaching, or two, quit teaching. I chose the former, and six years later, I have a fair work–life balance and adore my job. The school I left was a fantastic school and now achieves some enviable results, but a huge proportion of excellent staff left. It reminds me of the analogy of the general who stands on a hill congratulating himself about the battle he has won while he looks at the bodies of his fallen soldiers lying over the valley. The war was won, but at what cost? It was a price I simply wasn't willing to pay.

Voices from the profession

David Preece, head of geography

I believe that workload is an equation of what we have to do and the time we have to do it. I don't like being forced to do sub-par work at the last minute, and I refuse – where possible – to generate that pressure for anyone else. Of course, I can't control all the tasks, but I can make a big difference to my team by creating the time and space to do it.

I wanted to try to shift the narrative as a new head of department, and had three real objectives: I wanted to create spaces where we could talk about teaching and learning, not admin; with three very different teachers and styles in the department, I wanted to have a sense of where we all were (or 'should be') to help simplify our work; I wanted to be able to build and enhance my strong belief in a culture of 'no surprises'.

But how did I do it? Before each term began, I went through the school's calendar and flagged up the main things that I needed to share. This was distributed as a termly agenda to my department, where some items went into a 'school' column – events like Parents' Evenings or significant impact events, and the major non-negotiable deadlines for assessment and reporting. Then some items went into a 'department' column – for example, common assessments, or field trips that we were leading. These tended to be important in driving our meeting and work focus and went in separate from the whole school stuff, both in terms of our ownership of it and in terms of the solidity of the deadline! We then had a column for key things to focus on in each meeting. We've had student-focused discussions and pedagogy-focused discussions, and even planned fieldwork exercises together. This is also a time where responsibility can be shared – who is leading the meeting component, and what do they need to prepare?

This sets the overall framework of the term, together with a brief overview of the term's key challenges and success criteria. I don't want to be the only one who knows what we're trying to do, or what success looks like – then there are no surprises.

It rarely varies. If I do my job right, then there is no need for us to react and firefight to change situations and needs. If something comes up that we haven't anticipated, we can obviously add it in – but that's quite rare.

Each week, I send out a meeting agenda. It'll have the main ideas and outcomes that have previously been defined by the termly agenda, and a couple of bullet points which summarise where we're at or what we are likely to be working on this week. This is sent out the week before the meeting, and helps people to plan the week ahead and manage their own workload as professionals. It takes about an hour of my time each week, but I think it's worth it.

With the key ideas sent out as an email, staff can read them in their own time, keep them on file, or come back with questions. In our meetings, people are much more 'present' – there is very little scribbling of notes and reminders of what needs to be done. Rather than cramming our meetings full of admin tasks, we have increasingly been able to have real conversations about teaching, learning and students.

I can't change what needs to be done – but this mechanism enables people to plan 'when' they do things and to get control of their own workload. We have genuinely built a culture of no surprises, and I'm very proud of that.

Julia Childs, key stage 4 English teacher

I would describe my experiences of being a part-time teacher as a bit like the curate's egg: good in parts. I retrained to teach in my 30s and the ability to work part-time over the years helped me feel able to juggle work and motherhood reasonably successfully. As my children have grown, I have continued to work part-time, this time for health reasons. My hidden disability is becoming more troublesome as I age, and this working pattern enables me to pace myself and to schedule medical appointments on non-working days. In many ways, I am grateful to work part-time.

However, managing my workload is very challenging. My current job was advertised as a full-time role and I am doing it in half that time. I learned very quickly, for the sake of my body and soul, to set limits on the amount of time I am prepared to spend in school. So, I have regular working hours, which are entirely set by myself. I am still working way beyond my paid hours (roughly a day extra a week), and it has been commented upon that I am often in school at 'stupid o'clock'. However, I find my self-imposed working pattern to be manageable and it helps me to delineate a little between home and work. I never take marking home. The downside of keeping such regular hours is that sometimes others assume that I am being paid for all of them. In fact, I was once timetabled for a morning when I do not 'officially' work but am always around school.

I have learned to counteract this by keeping my door shut and by displaying my timetable clearly, with my non-working hours greyed out. I have also been known to work in the dark when I really don't want to be disturbed! I am getting better at politely reminding others of my non-working days and letting them know that I will reply to emails the following day. It definitely helps that my working days are split across the week. It means that I don't miss too much and so feel more 'present' and part of the team.

I am certain that working part-time has limited my career progression. I do not know anyone in leadership who works less than full-time and I am often asked if I will consider working more hours. It's then that I have to remind leaders that I work part-time for a reason. So, for me, working part-time is now a necessity, which is sometimes frustrating. This is my reality, though, and I am making the best of it.

Louis Everett, assistant head of teaching and learning

I have seen too many brilliant young teachers leave the profession since my PGCE in 2013. Why did they leave the profession? Workload was a major reason for some of these losses.

Now it is worth saying, like so many teachers, I am a self-confessed workaholic. If it were up to me, I would probably still be sitting in school talking about our key stage 3 curriculum. So it was not unheard of for me to work into the early hours as an NQT, with a large stack of marking. Luckily, school leaders are now beginning to realise that we do not need to be so reliant on time-inefficient, comment-heavy marking. More and more schools are altering their whole school marking policies, and my use of verbal feedback has convinced me that it is a unique opportunity to provide more nuanced subject-specific feedback within an academically rigorous history curriculum.

When I reflect back, I can see that my old reliance on 'individualised' comment-based marking was often ironically very generic! 'Explain further', 'good conclusion', 'more detailed evidence needed'. These 'individualised' comments are pretty meaningless without didactic instruction. Verbal feedback can empower us as subject experts to provide nuanced instruction to develop pupils' writing specific to the requirements of our discipline. I set about attempting to standardise my department's marking policy, to try to lower their workload whilst also improving the quality of their feedback.

I started off by telling them that I wanted no more written comments. Instead, when reading pupils' work, we have a piece of paper or maybe a slide open on PowerPoint, where we can jot down the common errors to feed back to the whole class verbally. This includes common spelling and grammatical errors. I was inspired to try this after reading the blogs of Joe Kirby and Ben Newmark. I wanted pupils to see their exercise books as a working document and to be able to constantly add to and correct their own notes as their knowledge was clarified.

Coding of marking has also totally changed my department's workload. As I read, I jot down regular errors or elements of pupils' writing that impress me. I give each comment a number and write either GD1 or T1, depending on whether I am praising work or setting a target. This is often used at A level, where the feedback given tends to be more precise, so why not use it at GCSE and key stage 3? When used alongside verbal feedback, modelling and redrafting, this can be effective and takes far less time than long written comments that make little impact.

Modelling and redrafting is, for me, the most vital bit of verbal feedback. As subject experts, we have the ability to model for pupils how they should write, analyse a source, quote from a historian, write a concise introduction, communicate their argument, etc. Verbal feedback has enabled me to model to pupils how I would like them to write, before allowing them time to practise this themselves and redraft their work. This is incredibly simple but equally powerful. It saves a huge amount of time and produces much better work.

The recent shift in attitude to marking is a unique opportunity to reject high-workload, low-impact, lengthy written comments in favour of nuanced, subject-specific feedback that can be understood and applied in a meaningful way by pupils. For those of us in school leadership positions, it is our responsibility to make the most of this shift and solve the workload crisis.

Eleanor Ridley, year 6 teacher

When I returned from maternity leave, I knew I needed to reduce my workload. So I set about this practically straight away, by trying to focus on aspects of my practice that I could control rather than on those I couldn't. Therefore, I set myself measurable targets. I had usually worked 65 hours a week before I left, and I was returning on 0.6 FTE (full-time equivalent); if I continued working proportionally at the same rate, that would have meant 39 hours a week. I would happily work a 50-hour week for teaching, so in proportion that would be a 30-hour week. On a good week now, I manage to get it down to 34 hours, so I am getting closer to my 30-hour target.

The most effective strategy I've used for reducing the hours spent on schoolwork (which is slightly different from workload) is simple. I write my 'To Do List', make a guess as to how long the tasks will sensibly take, and then I write down the start time and end time as I work on each task. At the end of each task, I do a quick evaluation of the strengths and weaknesses from a workload point of view.

After a few weeks of doing this, I had dramatically reduced the following: flitting between tasks; adding extra details that didn't also add impact; accidentally reading stories on MSN news when opening a new window, and spending ages looking for worksheets which clearly didn't exist online! What this strategy does is force you to notice any minutes you spend off task or on futile exercises. It doesn't change the workload that you are given; it just makes you manage the workload you have more efficiently.

Another valuable strategy I have used is to work in bulk: a former colleague pointed out that it is much more efficient to do certain tasks in bulk – for example, spelling. As the testing format and sheet that we send the spellings home on is the same every week, it is more efficient to find a time at half term to do six weeks in one go, as you won't waste time re-opening all your resources each week: you can cut and paste and build up a momentum. I would rather spend an hour-and-a-half on it at half term than 30 minutes on it each week, because it means I get extra weekly time to myself.

I think one problem is that whenever anyone suggests to a teacher that they need to work more efficiently, it's very easy to resent the comment and point out (rightly) that the volume of work expected is unmanageable. However, it is also true that we haven't, as a profession, been trained to be efficient, probably because we're not generating a monetary profit. To be 'Outstanding' educators, we need to be pragmatic as well as idealistic, so we spend our work time on value-added activities. This needs to happen at all levels, including that of class teacher.

Kat Howard, assistant principal
Teaching is just hard, so they say. You get the holidays, so they say. And it's all too simple to dismiss our profession as a given, a beast of its own creation, when it's far more complicated than that.

In reality, start points and end points of our roles are blurred at the edges, as we plan at our kitchen tables while others sleep, or at weekends when others do whatever people who work a nine-to-five do of a weekend. We watch sunshine from through the window as we mark exam papers, or buy Christmas presents in January whilst the feeling of Christmas stings fresh in our minds. We work hard to beat the clock, because at times it seems that the only way to master teaching is to try to outwit it – and what a predicament that can become.

Workload is more than planning, marking and wading through a swamp of emails of an evening: it is what good teaching without shortcuts is based upon, if we are to believe the narrative. In fact, managing workload is an intrinsic part of being a teacher, and always has been. To attempt to find a silver bullet to lessen the workload seems impossible and would have some calling us downright lazy. How dare we try to do less, when education and a firm grasp of knowledge demands exactly the opposite? And in the meantime, we continue to tick from the list, without really ever entirely knowing where the end of the list got to.

I would argue that workload isn't about that list, but about how schools use our time as teachers. In some schools, I have had the lightest of working weeks and been thoroughly miserable, and yet I have been all too happy to work significantly beyond the 40-hour utopian dream whilst employed in other schools because it felt like I had a sense of balance. How could that be so? It was because my time was truly valued by the school, and it was spent in the right way. This is as fundamental to teacher workload as just cutting stuff in half or making grand claims that actually just create pockets of work in different places.

Ask a teacher to plan and mark in isolation, and they'll feel unfulfilled and lacking any sense of collegiality. Ask a teacher to tap in column after column of data six times a year, and they'll resentfully master Excel spreadsheets and start wondering why they didn't become an accountant. Ask a teacher to log behaviour incidents in abundance every day, and they'll ponder over their future as a typist. None of these tasks is what teaching is about or what it sets out to achieve. Instead, draw teachers together to discuss the perils and pitfalls of their subject, so they might strategise against the common misconceptions that students may make; give time to teachers to share their knowledge and experience the magic as they talk over the depths of their specialism; present teachers with ownership and autonomy over what they need to develop as subject experts in their field, allowing them to spend time refining what they already know and working out what they do not yet know.

If we cherish teachers as the intellects of their art, and utilise their time as such, instead of giving them tasks that remove them further and further from their craft, then we will redefine teacher workload as something very purposeful indeed.

What can I do?

The research and voices from the profession make it clear: the workload in teaching can be like climbing a mountain – but there are ways to deal with it and make it manageable. However, it starts at the top. If you are a middle leader, who constantly feels like you are telling your staff to do things, there is another way. Are your department meetings as productive as they can be? If they are mainly taken up by admin and notices, then building a termly department agenda – which is a collaborative working document with all of the deadlines and admin notices on it – could free up more time to do the things that will really reduce workload, such as marking and moderating together or collaborative resource making and planning. It is also important that your staff know why they are being asked to complete things: absolute transparency will lead to a culture of 'no surprises' and total buy-in from your staff.

As marking is one of the biggest strains on teachers, change your focus to feedback. Books should not contain more writing from the teachers than pupils. Take the focus off the constant reliance on written feedback and instead use a range of different methods to provide students with the guidance, challenge and validation they need. As mentioned in the previous chapter, buying a verbal feedback stamp has allowed me to circulate the classroom while pupils are working, have a conversation with them and stamp their book. They then bullet point the feedback I have given them, underneath the stamp. They can use this feedback as a reminder for self-assessment or peer assessment at the end of the lesson, to help them judge their own or one another's work.

Marking codes are also another great time saver, and these can be put together in your department to ensure that errors and success criteria relevant to your subject are covered. In addition, whole class feedback sheets can be hugely successful, as often students will make similar mistakes, so the feedback sheets stop the need to constantly write the same comment. I particularly like using the type that gives a space to write down the names of pupils in the class who have done well in the task or to replicate some of their exceptional work. It is a real confidence boost for them and promotes better discussions in the class about why that piece of work was exemplary. Coloured dot marking is also another great idea that has sped up my marking. You give each student a different coloured dot sticker and then produce a key on the board showing what their feedback is. They can then record this and action it. Victoria Hewett, geography teacher and author of *Making it as a Teacher* (2019), has long been an advocate of the 'Feedback not Marking' approach, and she shared her wisdom about her experiences.

> Marking – it's been a contentious issue amongst educators for a number of years. The expectations to assess, comment and feed back to students both on paper and verbally started to spiral, and when triple marking as suggested by David Didau was so wrongfully interpreted, expectations were further exacerbated. For me it reached a point in 2014/15 when marking work simply became unsustainable and so I started to research alternatives to the traditional comment-based approach.
>
> It quickly became apparent that assessment was far more than reading work, commenting on it and expecting a student response. It's all part of a cycle of feed-up (setting, modelling and clarifying expectations),

feedback (assessment and response) and feedforward (action on feedback).

It's also important to recognise that feedback comes in many forms, the most obvious being verbal or written feedback from the teacher to the student. But we must also acknowledge and appreciate the feedback provided by students through their actions and behaviour, their verbal contributions and the comments they provide one another. Feedback is more than just marking work; it's clarification, it's assessment, it's approval and it's valuable. Take the time to carefully consider how and when feedback is provided, by planning backwards from the end, whether that be the topic, term or key stage. Doing so completely changed the way I plan, teach and assess, whilst also massively reducing my workload.

As Victoria explains, using different forms of feedback, rather than just sitting and spending hours doing traditional marking, can revolutionise your workload. There are examples of marking code sheets and whole class feedback sheets, such as the type Victoria advocates, at the end of this chapter.

Sometimes, however, pieces of individual work do need to be marked, such as GCSE exam answers or mock papers. With mock papers, small hacks such as marking the same question in all of your papers before going on to the next one will knock quite a bit of time off your marking, as you will not have to keep switching between marking criteria. If some of your in-class assessments can be changed to an online quizzing format, this will also be much quicker, as the computer will mark it for you. This is great for knowledge quizzes or quick comprehension activities, but for subjects like English, where there are long essay questions or pieces of creative writing, it can be much more difficult. This is where training students on how to peer assess thoroughly and properly can help to fight that marking workload. Over the last two years, I invested a huge amount of time ensuring that my GCSE class completely understood the GCSE mark schemes for their Language and Literature papers. I used examples from our class to demonstrate what each band answer looked like and why an answer would achieve that band. Then, we would all sit a timed exam question regularly in class – including me. Once the time was up, everybody would be given a response at random to grade after watching me live-mark one on the visualiser. It can be a bit nerve-wracking putting yourself out for scrutiny like this, but the students really appreciated that I was walking the walk, not just talking the talk. Obviously, this saved time, as previously I would have had to take all these responses home and mark them, whereas now I would just glance over them to check I agreed with the band the response had been placed in.

Of course, marking is not the only demand on our time. It is easy to get overwhelmed by the constant deadlines we have in schools. It is important to be able to step back and ask yourself: 'What is important? What will be checked?' Try to train yourself to not sweat the small stuff. How many times have you spent hours on a task only to have it cursorily glanced over and then forgotten about? A fantastic tip from Jodie Lopez on Twitter (@jodieworld) is to get yourself a three-tier in-tray on your desk and split your workload into this. The top tray is urgent and of direct benefit to students, so should be done first. The middle tray is of direct benefit to students and non-urgent, so should be done next, and the bottom is of no direct benefit to students, so can be done as and when you have time. The weekly aim is to have cleared the top tray by a Friday and then to triage the middle and bottom ones.

Managing workload is about having a clear understanding of our own working style and our driver behaviours, as they have a massive impact on what we do. We may be driven by our longing to seem strong, to make it look like we work hard or to try to please others. While these drivers can help us keep the purpose for what we are doing foremost in our mind, they can also exacerbate feelings of stress and pressure and can impede our ability to cope with our workloads. For many, compartmentalising what needs to be done in lists or trays will instantly make it seem more manageable, as they are very visible and measurable ways to show progress and achieve tangible things.

It is also important not to try to reinvent the wheel too much. The internet, if used well, can make it seem like you are part of a giant staffroom full of other like-minded and generous professionals who are keen to collaborate and share ideas. The wealth of resources is unbelievable. In my own subject, English, for example, Stuart Pryke (@ SPryke2) has an open access Dropbox where he saves all his high-quality lessons and resources, so time-poor teachers can use and adapt them for their own classes. There are teachers openly sharing their resources and expertise online for free on blogs or Twitter, for every subject – you just need to look for them.

Although workload is a very real problem, some of its potency in grinding down staff comes from the mind, in the guise of the dreaded teacher guilt. Teacher guilt happens when you feel like there is always more you want to do or could be doing for your students, if only you had the time to get it done. Yet you don't and never will. You send yourself crazy with thoughts that you may be a bad teacher because you haven't managed to do XYZ, or even worse, you compare yourself to other inspirational teachers who seem as if they have it all sorted. Chances are they are struggling as much as you and also have thoughts like this.

This pursuit to subscribe to the toxic cult of perfectionism is pernicious and dangerous. It is important to remember all the amazing things you ARE doing, not what you COULD be doing. You will have influenced and helped countless students, who remember you fondly. This is sometimes easily forgotten, though it shouldn't be. Like many of you, I have received some gorgeous cards and letters from pupils over the years and have always kept them in scrapbooks. Last year, after a tough term, I decided to create a display of some of them behind my desk in my classroom. Now, if I am having a bad day, I turn around and read some of these. It has become an instant positivity pick-me-up and drives me to carry on, knowing that while I may not have done everything on my 'To Do List', what I am doing is making a difference.

If you are struggling with how to manage your time effectively, you are not alone. According to recent research by Kogon, Merill & Rinne (2016), which measured productivity of 350,000 employees from all over the world, more than 40 per cent of time at work is spent on unimportant activities. This juggling of multiple tasks leaves people overwhelmed and stressed, spending time working on things that seem important, but which in reality are not. When this happens, the reactive part of our brain barges in and rushes tasks, boosting our dopamine because we are feeling busy and energetic. But at the end of the day, when we look back on how we spent our time, we can see that whole days can be wasted on doing trivial tasks that will make little or no difference to pupils. Instead, it is about developing a more conscious approach and spending time on what is important, not urgent.

Stephen Covey's Time Management Matrix can help with this, as rather than just listing what needs to be done, it helps to sort each task you need to do according to how urgent and important it is. It sorts tasks into four quadrants to help you decide on when tasks need to be completed and where your focus should be. Quadrant 1 focuses on any unforeseen events or problems that need to be dealt with immediately, such as a parental complaint. Things that fall into this quadrant should be dealt with proactively to avoid later problems. Tasks that fall into Quadrant 2 may not be urgent, yet most of our time should be spent working on the tasks that fall here, as they are more strategic, such as curriculum plans. If we are not managing our workload effectively, much of our day can be taken up with tasks that fall into Quadrant 3. These minor, urgent tasks, such as data inputting or answering emails, can constantly keep you busy but distract you from the things that really make a difference. Why not try to delegate these or allocate just an hour of the day to doing these? It will mean that much more of your time is spent in a more productive way. The final quadrant is full of the types of tasks that we tend to waste a lot of our time on, such as tidying up or filing things away. We need to cut these tasks to a minimum, as they just allow the more important tasks to build, creating the illusion that we are losing control.

Figure 6: Covey's Time Management Matrix (Covey, 1989)

	Urgent	Not Urgent
Important	1. Critical issues 2. Emergency work 3. Last-minute obligations	1. Important goals 2. Strategic tasks 3. Long-term projects and relationships
Not Important	1. Incoming mail and calls 2. Minor issues 3. Other people's queries	1. Routine tasks 2. Distractive talks 3. Time-killing activities

Finally, when it comes to workload and prioritising tasks, remember the golden rule: if it isn't directly for the benefit of the children, then ask 'Why are we doing it?' and 'Will it make a difference to the learners?' If the answer to any of these questions is unclear, don't do it. Think of your moral purpose. I am sure it isn't locked inside a spreadsheet or box-ticking exercise.

Figure 7: Example of a class marking code for English

Marking Code

Symbol	Meaning	Symbol	Meaning
Sp.	Spelling	>>	Expand on this
Gmr	Grammar error	BMF	Be more formal
?	What do you mean?	^	Missing word
/	New sentence	||	This doesn't make sense
//	New paragraph	w/o	Word order
*	Explain this point	T	Tenses
✓	Good	✓✓	Excellent
P	Presentation	U	Underline

Figure 8: Example of class marking code for English GCSE

Reading Targets:

1. Always use examples to back up the point that you make to show how you know.
2. Use the PEA format to help you to structure your analysis and to support you in hitting a C grade.
3. Make sure that your explanations are full and detailed. This will help you to push past C grade analysis.
4. Always explain your points – think because…
5. Always put quotes into speech marks.
6. Make sure that you use lots of detail in analysis – remember 'a lot about a little'.
7. Even though you are being marked for reading, secure spellings and sentence structures.
8. You need to write more under timed conditions.

Writing Targets:

1) Extend your range of punctuation to securely use : ; () … ! for effect.
2) Secure use of homophones, in particular their/they're/there.
3) Always use the word 'and' – don't use symbols.
4) Secure your use of commas in sentences for second clauses and lists.
5) Ensure that your work is split into appropriate paragraphs.
6) Secure punctuation at the end of your sentences to ensure that you end all sentences correctly.
7) Make sure that you use capitals for all names and places.
8) Plan your work effectively to ensure that it is well structured and there are links between paragraphs.
9) Experiment with vocabulary choices to avoid repeating the same phrases.
10) Always proofread your work. Check that it says what you actually want it to say.
11) Secure your use of apostrophes to ensure accuracy.
12) Make sure that all of your ideas are fully developed.
13) Keep your tenses secure – avoid slipping between past and present.
14) Extend and elaborate on your ideas with much more detail in order to aim for B/A and A* grades.
15) Complete all tasks that are set in class.
16) Develop your writing to include more language techniques.
17) Copy down spellings accurately to get it right the first time and then every time after that.

Figure 9: Whole class feedback sheet (a)

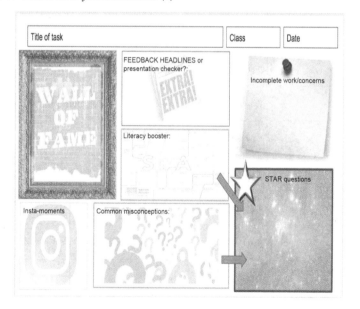

Figure 10: Whole class feedback sheet (b)

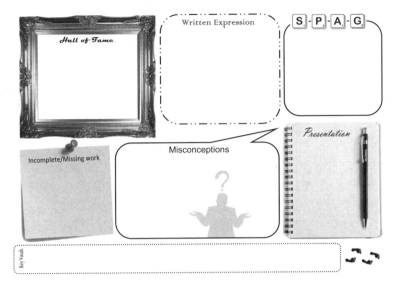

Chapter 3
Reason to leave #3: Whose fault is it anyway?
The pressure to secure results

The context

Every year, the papers write about the stress students are feeling about their impending SATs or GCSE exams, and, of course, it is a valid concern. However, many people forget that this is an extremely stressful situation for teachers also. Every year, it feels like you pour your heart and soul into your exam classes, constantly marking exam questions and making resources to challenge and inspire them. You devour the Examiners' Reports and scour the exam board website to find tips on how to achieve that elusive grade 9, desperate to give the kids the best chance possible to achieve amazing results. But when it comes to the actual exams, teachers have no control. It is over to the students, and this can be where the terror begins.

After the last exam, the stress disappears for a while and we spend time celebrating with the students at their leavers' assembly and their proms…but as August creeps towards us, the pressure comes back with a vengeance, and for some teachers, there are a lot of sleepless nights in the run-up to results day. But why is this the case? Surely the results that students get are mostly a reflection of the hard work, or lack thereof, that the pupils themselves have put in. Increasingly, schools are holding teachers to account for exam results, and it is causing some to consider leaving the profession.

Of course, having high expectations of your students is important, but some teachers feel like they are expected to perform miracles and that they may be blamed personally for the grades the students achieve if students don't do as well as they were expecting to. Essentially, this obsession with results stems from the marketisation of education that came from Margaret Thatcher's neoliberal ideology of schools competing with one another for student numbers and from the introduction of school league tables. The whole ethos of education in the UK changed: teachers were no longer just seeking to inspire students and imbue them with a passion for their subject. Education became a commodity – a commodity that could help the country compete on the global skills market (Shukry, 2017; Hargreaves and Shirley, 2012).

This marketisation of education also heralded the start of performance management targets for teachers, where the 'best' teachers have the most progress in their classes and exam results are high-stakes leverage in discussions on pay progression. Many top education trade unions state that any pay decisions should be based on appraisal outcomes and teacher standards – not numerical objectives – with the National Education Union stating that if exam results are used, 'it's accepted that account will be taken of anything outside your control affecting the outcome' (National Education Union, 2018). Yet many teachers are still being judged on their results and Progress 8 residuals and have been denied pay progression because of what their students achieved. Anyone who works in a school knows that students are not just defined by numbers on a slip of paper; they are so much more than that. So why should teachers be defined by it?

It's a pressure that so many teachers feel, from both their schools and parents. A teacher writing in the 'Secret Teacher' column in the *Guardian* newspaper (2018a) spoke of the feeling that fingers would be pointed at them if results were not as expected:

Many students and parents believe that it is the teacher's job to get a child good grades, whether or not they make an effort. If they do badly, or misbehave, that is your fault for making your lessons boring.

This kind of blame game can make parents' evening a night of dread, where teachers are on edge about the very real possibility that parents may blame them for their child's performance.

It seems these feelings are shared nationwide across the profession. In 2012, the Association of Teachers and Lecturers conducted some research with its members which revealed that 35 per cent felt that their professional integrity could be compromised as a result of the constant pressure to secure better results, whether that was through constantly coaching pupils through test papers, providing after-school sessions and one-to-one tuition, or even attending exam board seminars to impart some inside knowledge to their classes in a quest to help them get ahead. Almost 2300 malpractice offences were committed by staff in educational institutions offering OCR exams between 2012 and 2016. Most of the teachers committing the malpractice were accused of providing 'improper assistance' (the *Guardian*, 2012, 2018d) by helping students to achieve their grades by re-doing coursework or controlled assessment elements until students achieved the required grade.

Obviously, cheating is wrong and undermines the profession completely, but to stop things like this happening, the toxic culture that is pushing normally ethical professionals to commit acts that go against the very bedrock of fairness and idealism at the heart of teaching needs to be examined. The increased accountability and obsession with judging teachers' performances based on results is infecting our schools and causing an epidemic of mental illness in both students and staff.

For the passionate teacher, who enjoys fostering a love and curiosity for knowledge in their subject, having their teaching and learning confined by the parameters of exam-oriented teaching can belittle and de-professionalise. Studies have shown that this narrowing of the curriculum resulting from test-based accountability regimes in schools has a negative effect on students, as the lessons become very didactic and teacher-led, with less time for students to test their skills and knowledge independently (Ro, 2018; Slomp, 2008). The emotional impacts on teachers due to this kind of pressure cannot be denied. It can sometimes feel like living under a magnifying glass of scrutiny and accountability; it isn't hard to see why some teachers decide that enough is enough and that they deserve more recognition than just the numbers their class receives once a year.

It seems Ofsted also agrees. In 2018, when Amanda Spielman set out her vision for the new inspection framework to school leaders in Newcastle, she stated that 'for a long time, our inspections have looked hardest at outcomes, placing too much weight on test and exam results when we consider the overall effectiveness of schools'. She continued that this 'has increased the pressure on school leaders, teachers and indirectly on pupils to deliver perfect data above all else' (the *Guardian*, 2018c). Instead, judgements in today's inspection framework are much more rounded and focus more on the quality of education provided at a school, including whether the curriculum has a clear intent and how the curriculum is implemented. Unfortunately, some schools are still focusing too heavily on outcomes, and that pressure is still filtering down to teachers. I know, as I have felt it too.

As this book was going to press, GCSE and A level examinations had just been cancelled because of school closures as part of the plan to battle COVID-19. Instead, grades were to be awarded to students based on previous data and school performance, teacher predictions and rank ordering of pupils. Perhaps this could create a seismic shift in the way we assess pupils in the future, with head teachers hoping that this could be an opportunity to change assessment to a less 'brutal' process (*TES*, 2020a). Former English teacher and Association of School and College Leaders (ASCL) union General Secretary, Geoff Barton, said:

> Teachers are experts in their subjects, they know these qualifications inside out, they know their students, and they have the professional skills to assess them

accurately. We do not subscribe to the notion that exams are the only credible way of assessing qualifications. (Edexec, 2020)

If in the aftermath of this pandemic, the way we assess students is changed in the way Barton hints at, it could stop many more teachers from feeling under so much pressure that they are faced with feeling the need to make the monumental decision to leave the classroom.

My story

Like most teachers, I look forward to result's day every year, but can never help but feel a slight trepidation, which usually involves a few sleepless nights and butterflies on the way in that morning. For many years, I had taught the lower sets and I loved seeing them find a passion for English that they had never previously felt, but I would rarely witness the euphoric highs of students opening their envelopes and achieving those top grades. But in 2014, I was particularly nervous, as I had taught a top set since year 7 and was putting huge pressure on myself, thinking that if their results were sub-standard, as their only teacher throughout the whole of secondary school, I would be solely responsible.

Arriving at school that morning, the atmosphere was strangely quiet, and I bumped into the recently appointed head teacher at the door. I didn't even need to ask; it was clear from his grim face that results were not good and that the school would be in trouble. With a sense of dread, I scanned the spreadsheet and examined my class. Most had achieved what I would have expected, but there were some strange results that almost brought me to tears. It seemed so unfair. I knew that the students would be upset and that I had to be there to tell them everything was going to be okay.

It was in this situation that I found myself catapulted to head of department only two weeks later. Results in my school were the worst they had ever been, and the school was looking for an overnight improvement. The pressure was on.

It was the era of controlled assessments, and the first priority was to ensure that all students went into the exam with the highest possible grades in these, as they were worth 40 per cent of the final grade. As I taught 3 year 11 classes, administering and marking all of these was a huge undertaking, and the pressure to help students more than I should have was palpable. Yet I knew that this was unethical and that I wasn't willing to compromise my integrity in this way.

But it felt like every new week brought a new spreadsheet checking progress, a new meeting with members of my team to check that they were intervening with key students, and a new grilling from senior leaders to demand that we do more. Cheating began to look attractive. I knew I had to get out. So I made the difficult decision to leave the school I loved mid year, abandoning my year 11 classes and a form I had been with for five years. I knew that exam results were important, but I was losing the love of teaching, as it seemed that schools just judged students and teachers on their progress and what numbers they achieved.

Voices from the profession

Andrew Cartwright, head of English

I have been a HoD for the past nine years, and, without exception, every year has seen the same feelings of dread and anxiety as the inevitable examination analysis meetings which are scheduled in my diary creep slowly closer...

I teach in a large academy in North West England; a school that serves a community that is in the top quartile of the most disadvantaged areas in the country. Our cohort remains quite stagnant in terms of ability on entry, with roughly 12 per cent being classified as 'high ability' and 45 to 50 per cent classified as 'low ability'. Many of those students have no key stage 2 scores at all, and, for some strange reason, they are meant to perform higher at key stage 4 than their peers. Apart from one or two years of immense success, where outcomes were significantly above FFT50, we achieve roughly in line with FFT50 every year – sometimes just below that, though close. As with most schools, however, if our cohorts are very low ability on entry, our hard work and perseverance may not match the final outcomes. Of course, those outcomes are also always negatively impacted upon by those students termed as 'outliers' – the 10 per cent of our cohorts who are school-refusers or suffer significant child protection or emotional issues and we simply don't see them through years 10 and 11. No matter the interventions put in place and no matter the high quality teaching we deliver on a daily basis, we struggle to reach these students. I really cannot praise my team enough for the 'extra miles' they give to support, nurture and challenge our students to achieve to the best of their ability.

But every August and September, these efforts all pale into insignificance when we are faced with the same barrage of questions at the analysis meetings: 'What did you do this year to offset any potential areas of underperformance from last year?'; 'Why did teacher A, with 11A4, not achieve as well as or better than teacher B with 11B4?'; 'Tell me why your interventions didn't work effectively?'; 'If your year 11 class performed well, why didn't every other year 11 class perform to the same level?'; 'Why have your outcomes stagnated at 60 per cent grades 4 to 9 every year?' The absolute killer, that I've sadly heard twice now, is: 'Are you still the right man for the job?' The meetings always end with the same deadline date – usually three days – to create and share a departmental action plan that will absolutely guarantee higher outcomes for the following year.

In those moments of crushing defeat and anxiety, the whole role seems pointless and unachievable. I am also expected to discuss underperformance with staff, even though I don't perceive there to be any: colleagues I work with have given all that they can to support students, to revise with them, to challenge them and nurture them. I know, even as the results come in every August and before I have to analyse the data and write the annual departmental action plan, that we will always be stuck between a rock and a hard place. Ofqual's all-consuming focus on statistical outcomes means that no matter what we do, we'll never shift a cohort that is, for the most part, significantly below the ability range on entry. To succeed in Gove's world of 100 per cent terminal examinations and Language and Literature for all it just seems an impossible task. Progress 8 and statistical outcomes are simply another stick to beat us all with.

I came into teaching quite late in life, having previously been employed in the Armed Forces. I have been at the same school for 14 years. I love the place and love teaching the kids – as tough as some are – and will soon meet my eighth head in that time. I draw a metaphorical cattle train around the team, and we all move on together. A great team can help you cope with anything.

Anonymous, computer science teacher
When asked to reflect on my experiences of accountability for GCSE results, it brought back a lot of negative thoughts and feelings – something I now have to actively work hard at to keep at bay. GCSEs are important and I don't think anyone will deny that, but they are never more important than one's well-being and integrity, both of which were heavily compromised for me when taking through my second cohort. The thought of observations, predicted grades and any leadership responsibility for key stage 4 now fills me with dread because, whilst in my training year, I was left with no support in my department; the HoD left and was never replaced, and all the important decisions were left to me. How much support did I give students in their coursework? How high did I predict their grades? Apparently, my answers and approaches were never correct.

At times, I felt under pressure to go against exam board regulations, which I refused to do unless it was written in an email to me rather than said verbally. Of course, this never happened. My low predicted grades ended up initiating a long battle to prove that I deserved to pass my NQT year. No longer was my qualification based on my observations, lesson planning or student relationships. It was based on my predicted grades and the amount of 'support' I was perceived to be giving to 'my' year 11s. I put quotation marks around those words, as the school and I had different interpretations of them. At one point, I was asked to explain results for a photography class...I have never taught photography.

The amount of pressure for these grades became too much for me to handle, and I was signed off – something I never thought would happen. I was invited to a health review, which I cried most of the way through, and my line manager answered most of the questions directed at me. Still, it seemed somewhat positive...Until a few hours later, that is, when I was at home and got a notification from the NQT manager. This told me that my report, which had been written months ago, had been changed from an A to a C grade. So, on top of the guilt I felt for leaving my students, I felt really panicked about my teaching status. I saw my GP with the intention of having a certificate to be deemed fit to work, but he (rightfully) would not agree to it. I had made the decision months earlier to leave the school and had another job lined up, so I just needed to get through the last term.

When I did return, however, I was asked to resign or else risk not being able to teach in an English state school again. Fortunately, I had great support from my borough. I scraped through and moved on to a school that was much better for me. It does make me wonder, though, if all the angst would have been avoided had I just lied and predicted higher grades. Unfortunately, I think the answer is yes, which speaks volumes about the whole system.

Again, GCSE grades are important, and the high that you feel when students show appreciation for their successes is wonderful. However, there are so many factors that constitute this final grade, and it's just not as simple as the grade reflecting the quality of the teacher; far too much pressure and accountability are put on the teachers in my opinion. After all, they work incredibly hard and genuinely want the best for their students. Yet, at the end of the day, the results belong to the students, not to the teachers.

Speaking to external people really helped. I wish I had got into contact with the borough a lot earlier than I did. I also started reading again, which helped a lot – especially more light-hearted books that helped to take my mind off things. Quite a few of my other colleagues in the school also felt targeted, so speaking to others and having that nice bit of solidarity and support made me realise it wasn't my fault. You must keep in mind that it isn't you. I am a strong believer that it was the school, not the profession, as I am in a much better position in my new school.

Anonymous, former head of history

One Easter, I took over a department where results had been falling for a couple of years. Whilst I was not held accountable for that year's poor results, it was clear that the school expected me to turn them around – and fast. This was despite knowing that it was a challenging cohort. I had to fully resource the course, as the previous HoD hadn't left any SOWs or resources on the department shared drive. I had to plan and resource the whole GCSE course from scratch. The A level course was also in the same state, so I ended up switching to a board I knew to make it more manageable.

The results improved by 5 per cent, and whilst still under the national average, they were in line with other subjects across the school. Nevertheless, I was informed by letter that October that I was being denied pay progression on the basis that results were below the national average! This was not a specified target in my appraisal objectives, and most other classes were doing well. I remonstrated and was simply told that senior leaders were also being denied progression. I was stunned. I had made massive changes to the delivery of GCSE, and key stage 3 was being reviewed to make improvements. One year was simply not enough to give the massive turnaround that they were looking for.

I didn't deal with it well at the time, but with no support from any line manager, it was no surprise. I did try to be part of the solution, but nobody listened and I was put off applying for other jobs, as I worried about the accountability for results. In retrospect, I could have been more effective in my challenges. But if people ever find themselves in a situation like this, I would definitely recommend that they use the education support helplines and the unions to make a formal challenge.

Anonymous, SENCo (special educational needs coordinator)

As an NQT in my first school, I had a great SLT. They were always supportive and kind. They were very caring people who always seemed to have the best interests of their children in mind. As I came closer and closer to the end of spring term, I realised there was some rule-bending going on. Staff were not controlling controlled assessments properly: they were leaning over children and telling them what to write, or just writing it for them. When I questioned it, I was always met with a challenging tone. 'Do you not care about these kids? They would have a better life if we helped them here.' It all stemmed from the pressure put on the SLT to improve results – a pressure that was driven down to staff. We were a 'Special Measures' school with a relatively new leadership team, and the pressure was on to get results. I raised it several times with the head, but somehow, I always left the office feeling like I was overreacting, or just not experienced enough to understand. Eventually, however, I left the school.

Later on, as a SENCo, I was always very cautious about adhering to JCQ (Joint Council for Qualifications) regulations. It was my responsibility to make sure that the school was compliant, and I took it very seriously. I was made aware that the head teacher was bending the rules for certain students – students who were predicted high grades but who had struggled during their secondary schooling and students who had no diagnosed SEND (special educational needs and disability) but were unlikely to have made progress. When I challenged this via email, I was called for a meeting, where I was told in no uncertain terms that the decision was below my pay grade, that I mustn't really care about the difficult circumstances of our children, and that if I were older (I was 32) I would understand the need for results.

I was so upset. I decided to keep a log of every decision I made and verified it with another colleague, as I felt I couldn't trust the leadership team anymore. The desire for results had overtaken the desire for fair and equal access. Not only did it challenge the very precarious nature of exam access requirements, which can often be difficult to obtain for students that really need them, but it also gave these children a crutch. I left at the end of that year.

John Hodgson, academic and editor of *English in Education*
During the 11 years I worked at the end of the last century as head of the English department in a large rural comprehensive

school, uninformed political interference in the curriculum became an increasing annoyance. For many years, we had followed the AQA A level Literature course, which required students to submit eight essays and an extended project on the texts they had read. The students enjoyed the opportunity to research in their own time and to write creatively as well as analytically. It was a pleasure to work with them and to see their writing develop. The unwarranted decision in 1993 to reduce A level coursework to a token 20 per cent was a blow for thousands of teachers and students across the country.

Equally disturbing was the development of a culture of targets that positioned teachers merely as operatives in the examination industry and students as figures in league tables. At the beginning of each school year, I agreed assessment targets with the senior management team. Each year, our key stage 3 SAT results were moderate and slightly below target. But our GCSE results (for the same students two years later) always exceeded targets. So each year the department was congratulated on the 'value' it had 'added' to students during years 10 and 11. It was evident that there was no coherent progression of assessment from key stage 3 to GCSE, and I was increasingly irritated to be working in a system where students' achievement was marked only by a flawed external marking regime. As Williams & Williams (2017) argue, several aspects of English are best assessed by coursework. Teachers should have opportunities to meet regularly with colleagues to develop a professional community of practice as coursework assessors. This was one of the great strengths of the AQA A level Literature course (Hodgson and Greenwell, 2017).

The breaking point for me was an Ofsted inspection. This had a very different feeling from the HMI (Her Majesty's Inspector) visits to which I had become accustomed in my earlier career. HMIs would spend an entire period in one classroom, sometimes take part in the lesson, and speak to the teacher at the end. The Ofsted inspectors seemed less able to relate to the teachers and pupils or, indeed, to each other. They had been supplied by agencies working for Ofsted and had not previously worked as a team. At the end of the week, the English inspector, whose teaching experience had been largely in international schools abroad, recommended we try to improve students' vocabulary – an extraordinarily bland recommendation that was disconnected from any coherent subject pedagogy and showed no recognition of the efforts we made to increase students' cultural understanding (and thus their vocabulary) by a richly contextual study of literary and media texts.

So it was time to go. After working for 15 years in higher education and completing a PhD on adolescent literacy, I now write, research and edit an international journal. I still miss teaching.

What can I do?

The current system of education, all the way from primary school to university, is so entrenched in high-stakes assessments and exams that it may be impossible to avoid being affected by exam pressures and stress to some extent. This sense of powerlessness and being pressed by the weight of other people's expectations can be exhausting. However, developing some key coping strategies will help you survive this exam season and many more to come.

Firstly, you need to take control. When you are feeling stressed and anxious, it can seem like things are spiralling out of control and your mind is racing with negative thoughts and scenarios. Remember to breathe. Even just setting aside a few minutes a day to do some mindfulness techniques or breathing exercises will help shift your attention back to calm and the here and now, not 'what ifs?' There are hundreds of 'Ten-minute mindfulness' style meditation videos you can access for free online, but the one found on headspace.com is particularly calming and helpful. Visualisation exercises might also help with negative thought patterns. Imagine yourself in a happier place or immerse yourself in planning your next fun weekend or summer holiday – any thoughts of results day will hopefully go to the back of your mind. There is a mindfulness resource at the end of this chapter for you to try, but there is a wealth of activities you can try for free online.

Talking therapies like cognitive behaviour therapy (CBT) can also help to change the way we think and feel. Our thoughts, feelings and behaviour are all linked, and if we have negative thoughts, this can lead to feelings of stress and pressure that may make us behave in ways that are out of character. Negative and unrealistic thoughts about worst case scenarios in exams and about students, parents and school leaders blaming individual teachers will mean that the actual situation becomes skewed, so it is about trying to clear the fog and think rationally. For example, if our brains are constantly churning with the thought that we may be blamed for sub-standard exam results by middle or senior leaders, we need to recognise that these are unhelpful beliefs because, chances are, leaders in your school will know how hard you work and will appreciate your efforts. It is important that we recognise, observe and monitor the pressures we are putting on ourselves when it comes to exam results. Journaling our feelings using CBT techniques can also be helpful. Why not try the template at the end of the chapter to try to rationalise your thoughts?

Of course, it can be incredibly difficult to switch from the high mental activity of stress, and switching off for mindfulness, visualisation or journaling may seem impossible at this moment. But sometimes simply employing distraction techniques can help. Thoughts about school can be overwhelming and all-encompassing, but focusing your energies on a new hobby or something you've always wanted to do may help switch your focus. For me, I could lose myself in a book for hours on end, but others may find solace in exercise. Whatever you choose, it is important to fight stress by spending time on your own well-being – even if that means switching off and watching the football with a beer. This is hugely important as results day approaches, as thoughts of what may happen can dominate. You matter too. Without you, students would not have even been able to approach this exam. It's key that you remember that the contribution you are making to young people is vital, so you need to take care of yourself.

As the research and voices from the profession sections in this chapter show, exam stress and the pressure that comes from teacher accountability is very real, and it is important that we recognise that it exists. Millions of teachers up and down the country may be feeling the same way you are, and it is important to reach out to others, even just to voice how you are feeling and get some validation. This can be immensely reassuring and soothing. It can be difficult for people who are not in the profession to understand why teachers feel this level of responsibility for results, so speaking to fellow professionals and colleagues will help alleviate your fears and remind you that this too will pass.

Figure 11: Ten-minute meditation resource (Harvard University, 2016)

Add mindfulness to your day
in only 10 to 15 minutes

Here are 4 ways to add mindfulness to your schedule. Each way only takes 10 to 15 minutes of your time:

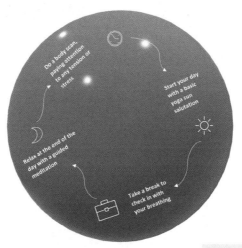

Do a body scan, paying attention to any tension or stress

Start your day with a basic yoga sun salutation

Relax at the end of the day with a guided meditation

Take a break to check in with your breathing

* Remember, consistency is key!

Figure 12: Rationalisation CBT resource

THOUGHT RECORD

1. Situation	2. Moods	3. Automatic Thoughts (Images)	4. Evidence that supports the 'Hot Thought'	5. Evidence that does not support the 'Hot Thought'	6. Alternative/Balanced thoughts	7. Rate moods now
Who were you with? What were you doing? When was it? Where were you?	Describe each mood in one word. Rate intensity of mood. Circle or mark the mood you want to examine.	What was going through my mind before I started to feel this way? What images or memories do I have in this situation?	What was the 'Hot Thought' that made you feel this way? What evidence supports your thought?	What logical evidence does not support this 'Hot Thought'?	Write an alternative or more balanced thought. Rate how much you believe each alternative or balanced thought.	Copy the moods from column 2. Now re-rate the intensity of each mood, as well as any new moods.

Chapter 4
Reason to leave #4: Juggling fire
Behaviour and attitude

The context

As we have seen, teachers choosing to leave the profession do so for a myriad of different reasons that take their toll over a sustained period. But for some teachers, the negative behaviour incidents and the disruptive attitude of some students are making their positions untenable. In the 'Factors affecting teacher retention: qualitative investigation research report' published by the DfE in 2018, teachers spoke about their dissatisfaction with pupil behaviour and how it hindered them in planning creative and engaging activities in lessons, causing them to feel disrespected. The attitude of pupils can have a huge influence on the well-being and job satisfaction of teachers. When students are motivated to do well and are respectful, teaching can be the most rewarding job in the world. Days can be full of euphoric highs and positivity, as we witness students 'getting it', but when there are constant low-level disciplinary issues, the daily grind of dealing with these can make teaching a chore and create additional workload with the need for logging of incidents and communication with parents.

Of course, teachers are not naïve; they know behaviour issues have always existed. After all, they were once students themselves! Recently, records from the 1970s and 1980s were unearthed in a primary school in Greenfield, Oldham, which detailed how youngsters were punished for a range of incidences of 'continual disruptive behaviour' and 'repeated acts of vandalism and indiscipline' (the *Daily Mail*, 2017). Yet half a century later, challenging behaviour is still one of the most difficult problems that teachers face in their everyday working lives. In fact, a survey by Education Support in 2018 revealed that 43 per cent of teachers said poor behaviour was a cause of physical and mental health issues they suffered. It is quite sobering and shocking to think that almost half of all teachers are suffering with the effects of disruptive behaviour in their classrooms, and it is therefore no surprise that so many become disaffected and consider leaving the profession.

People may mistakenly think that behavioural issues are mostly the problem of inexperienced practitioners, yet this is simply not the case. In a study that looked at mid-life teachers who were considering leaving the profession, many participants in the study mentioned the constant battle with disruptive behaviour as one of the key indicators in their dissatisfaction with teaching. One of the teachers interviewed stated: 'If you had a difficult class, you felt they were just throwing it back at you and weren't listening, weren't doing it properly. And you just felt thoroughly disillusioned' (Cooper and Mackenzie Davey, 2011). Experienced teachers I interviewed spoke of feeling like they were slowly being worn down, their love for the profession ebbing away. Even those who felt they had a good handle on behaviour management and had worked in more challenging contexts had become increasingly frustrated by the kind of behaviours that now seem to be accepted in many British classrooms.

It isn't just secondary teachers who find themselves dealing with behaviour issues either. Increasingly, primary colleagues are struggling to deal with the defiant and sometimes violent conduct of some of their pupils. In the report on reasons why people leave the profession conducted by the DfE in 2018, a teacher stated: 'we had children with significant behavioural difficulties, children who were probably acting out older sibling gang-related stuff. Children wanting to run the class themselves, very oppositional and defiant, very aggressive. This is [the] first time I have felt personally afraid' (DfE, 2018: 24).

So why is this continuing to happen, and is behaviour in schools getting worse?

According to a YouGov poll in 2018, the overwhelming majority of teachers believe that it is. In the poll, 57 per cent of teachers questioned said that they believed there had been a deterioration since 2013, with primary school teachers noticing the biggest difference. Many of the teachers questioned who felt the decline was more noticeable had been teaching more than five years, and cited issues such as bigger class sizes and budget cuts as possible reasons why this could be the case. But others felt that a lack of support from the SLT and parents or inconsistent application of whole school behaviour policies were key factors. A report by Dr Joanna Williams (Policy Exchange, 2018) later that year went on to suggest that there is an appetite among teachers for a tougher approach from schools, with behaviour management policy refresher sessions for all staff so that behaviour policies can be applied more robustly. Unfortunately, when policies are interpreted differently by staff in the same school, it can send mixed messages to students, which result in the rules becoming unclear or watered down.

An example of this was demonstrated in some recent CPD I witnessed. A series of signs displaying consequences were displayed around the school hall, and staff were given negative behaviour scenarios and asked to stand next to the consequence they felt was the most appropriate sanction for the behaviour. For each and every scenario given, there was a disagreement among staff as to what the consequence should be, despite the school having a clear behaviour policy and a chain of escalating consequences.

One scenario given was that a child had made a homophobic remark to his peer in a lesson. Many of the teachers in the session believed that the child should be sent straight out of the room for making this comment, rather than receiving a verbal warning, as this would send a message to the student the comment had been directed at and to the rest of the class that this kind of behaviour was completely unacceptable. Some other colleagues felt that a simple quiet word would suffice, and that if the behaviour persisted, then the child should be sent out of the room. Who was right? The school's policy stated that in the early stages of the consequences chain, pupils should be given the opportunity to make the right choice about their behaviour before being sent out, yet this does not send a helpful message to the victim of the abuse who has already suffered humiliation and hurt from the words the student chose to use. That is the difficulty with behaviour policies – it is impossible for them to take into account the wildly varying situations that teachers often find themselves in. The consequences can be quite general, and they are open to interpretation. As Tom Bennett wrote in his independent report on behaviour in schools, for a behaviour policy to be successful, it needs to have 'attention to detail and thoroughness' so that staff are completely clear about any sanctions they will be giving and about when to give them (Bennett, 2018: 7).

Even if policies are used consistently, there will be some occasions where senior leaders need to step in and support classroom teachers and middle leaders with behaviour when all the other avenues have been exhausted. Sometimes that support isn't provided as successfully as it should be, and in research by Ofsted (2019), teachers stated that they felt there was a lack of support from both school leaders and parents. The report recommended that 'leaders must support teachers to consistently implement behaviour policies' and 'should develop staff well-being by creating a positive working environment in which staff feel supported, valued and listened to'. Far too many teachers I interviewed spoke about how they had felt undermined by senior leaders who 'batted behaviour back to them' after they felt they had done all within their power to repair the relationship with the pupil.

Chris Keates, General Secretary of the NASUWT teaching union, believes that fashionable behaviour approaches such as restorative justice are contributing to this problem. She told the *Daily Telegraph* that although the principles of restorative justice are sound, senior leaders in school are misinterpreting the approach, viewing the meeting between the student and member of staff as the only consequence of the bad behaviour. Clearly, just having a meeting between a student and teacher, with a senior leader mediating, is not a sanction for bad behaviour, and this can result in the teacher being presented as somehow equally culpable as the child. This disempowers the teacher and erodes their authority. According to Keates:

> Good pupil discipline comes [from] having good leadership and making it clear that teachers have got to be respected and setting out clear expectations on pupil behaviour. Where that doesn't take place, that makes the job in the classroom for teachers more difficult. (the *Telegraph*, 2019)

During my research, a teacher I spoke to recalled a restorative justice meeting she had taken part in with a child who had consistently insulted her and behaved in a threatening manner. The head of year mediated and pointed the finger at the teacher, telling her in front of the pupil that the student's attitude was down to her mismanagement of the situation. All the while, the student smirked and laughed at her, knowing that she was not going to be held to account for her behaviour. The teacher told me that she felt so upset that she now rarely bothers to flag up behaviour incidents and lets a lot of things slide, as she knows the support will not be there if she does follow it up.

Another worrying sign in schools is the number of teachers who have reported being verbally or physically assaulted or faced with threatening behaviour from students. The Health and Safety Executive (HSE) defines workplace violence as 'any incident in which a person is abused, threatened or assaulted in circumstances relating to their work', and states that it can include verbal abuse or threats as well as physical attacks. Statistics show that teaching professionals face a higher than average rate of violence at work (NEU, 2019), with assaults in school rising by 72 per cent in the last four years (*Schools Week*, 2019). A survey by the NASUWT shockingly revealed that nearly one in four teachers were physically attacked by pupils at least once a week, with 29 per cent reporting that they had been hit, punched or kicked. One teacher, who was a former rugby player, said they were 'more protected against physical violence and verbal intimidation on the pitch' than they were as a teacher in a school (the *Independent*, 2019). Obviously, this is completely unacceptable. In any doctor's surgery or shop, signs are displayed stating that verbal and physical abuse towards staff will not be tolerated. Why is the same courtesy not extended to teachers? Instead, it seems like they are expected to just soldier on at the expense of their emotional well-being.

Figure 13: Number of assaults reported to police in secondary schools each year from 2015 to 2019 (Schools Week, 2019)

NUMBER OF ASSAULTS

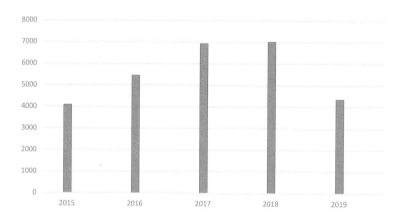

Although some may argue that assaults and violent behaviour are still rare in schools, I would argue that it is the persistent disruptive behaviour that is more detrimental to teachers' mental health. Yet despite this, permanent school exclusions for persistent disruptive behaviour, which still remains the most common reason for exclusions, have fallen for the first time in five years (DfE, 2019b). Obviously, school exclusions should always be a last resort, and data still show that there is a disproportionate number of school exclusions of certain pupils from English schools, such as Black Caribbean boys, Gypsy, Roma and Traveller children, children with special educational needs and those who are eligible for free school meals (DfE, 2019b).

However, not excluding children who are struggling with life in a mainstream school may leave many children in schools not having their needs met and being trapped in a cycle of negative behaviour patterns. Also, student behaviour in schools has a strong correlation with achievement, better teaching and learning and staff satisfaction (Bennett, 2017). Therefore, it is absolutely crucial for the sake of all pupils that schools create a culture where good behaviour is an expectation. Then, perhaps, more excellent teachers will not feel compelled to look for career alternatives outside of teaching.

My story

I have always enjoyed teaching the sparky, misunderstood pupils – the ones who seem to continuously misbehave and fight back against staff. That's probably because I was one of them. In secondary school, I didn't last the full five years. Instead, I was given an early bath (an expression often heard in football and sometimes used in the north for being excluded from school) in year 11, collected from my RE lesson in the last period of the day and told that I was going home and wouldn't be coming back. I wasn't unteachable by today's standards. I just had a disdain for authority and a steady insolence that seemed to erupt out of my mouth before a teacher had even finished speaking. It was so unlikely that I would eventually end up as a teacher myself that my old form teacher nearly choked on his coffee when I arrived back at my school, in my late 20s, to complete a placement as part of my PGCE. Therefore, it's no surprise really that I recognise this trait in others and see beyond it, as I know they're eventually going to be okay and will learn to control it.

It was with this background and longing to make a difference that I started my NQT year in a challenging school in a socio-economically deprived area; essentially, I was surrounded by kids who, like me, just needed a chance, some kindness and a consistent adult presence to guide them in the right direction.

I never really had many problems with behaviour, but I witnessed shocking instances of disruption and violence around the school. One of the worst was when a year 11 boy refused to leave a classroom and began to make threats to a young teacher. The teacher called a member of the SLT, who came to the classroom to diffuse the situation and, after reasoning with the pupil, had to get the rest of the students out of the classroom because the boy was acting in a volatile manner. The pupil then pushed the senior leader, who put his arms up to protect himself, and the boy bit a chunk from his arm. The teacher later required surgery. The most sickening thing about the whole incident, though, was the resistance to reporting the incident to the police, as it was felt that it might 'ruin the life chances of the boy'.

At another school, I was pushed by a girl and called a 'slut' in front of a classroom full of year 9 students. I had a reputation in the school as being a tough teacher. I was someone none of the kids messed with, as they knew that I had standards and that I stuck by those standards. Imagine my disdain, then, when I spoke to the curriculum leader after the incident, expecting them to intervene with the student and give her a punishment that I didn't have the authority to give, such as seclusion or a fixed-term exclusion. I was informed that other than a detention, his hands were tied. Obviously, exclusions are not always the answer and they shouldn't be doled out like lollipops to kids, but there needs to be a visible and serious consequence for an assault on staff. It was clear to the class that, as this girl was seen to get away with it, they could now behave however they liked, and the lessons with them for the rest of the year were some of the worst of my career.

While behaviour has never contributed to my wanting to leave the profession, it has certainly contributed to my stress levels. After working in challenging schools for much of my career, I have a vast range of behaviour management strategies in my repertoire, and my approach of firm expectations with a warm smile has meant that I am able to teach largely without disruption – but I still have my bad days. On these days, it's hard to remain positive, and I have found myself looking for other roles in education or opportunities to retrain, as the hurt can sting and resonate for a while. Many educators have the tendency to focus on the negative, as we are such perfectionists, but when I have days like this, I try to think logically about all of the positive interactions I have had that day, and they always outweigh the negative. This and the ability to reach out and change the mindset of some pupils who dislike school is what keeps me going.

Voices from the profession

Anonymous, head of English

I'd had a student in my form since year 7 and he'd always been a challenge. On a year 7 residential, he'd refused to engage with me for three days after I grabbed him by the hood to pull him out of a dangerous situation he'd previously been warned about, and the relationship hadn't really improved by year 9. One day, during a fire drill, I'd asked him to stop talking and also to get rid of his chewing gum. He defied me a couple of times, but after the final request, he took the gum out of his mouth and spat on me – all down my trouser leg. Revolted and mortified, I went to a senior member of staff and was told that I would have to deal with it myself, as the boy was a member of my form. It seemed to be viewed as a trivial misdemeanour. It wasn't the first time I'd felt unsupported, but it was the final straw, and that afternoon I began to look elsewhere for a job.

I wasn't a rookie teacher, not that that should make a difference anyway, but six years of teaching experience hadn't equipped me with the means to handle this kind of defiance, and there was no formal system in place in the school. Detentions were conducted by departments, and as far as I recall, we didn't have a means of sending students home for fixed-term exclusion that anyone other than more senior pastoral colleagues could employ. I was considered to be an effective teacher, I was a mentor for ITT and led a whole school initiative, but I had no power in this situation, which I believe would have been classed as an assault had it taken place in the street.

As it happened, I ended up working in a school where behaviour was generally much worse, but the difference was that there was always someone who would provide support. In the early days, there wasn't much in the way of a behaviour policy, but colleagues would step in. For example, I very soon found powerful allies in colleagues from the PE department, who would refuse to take boys out to represent the school in matches if they'd been badly behaved in class. This was a school where people looked out for one another and no teacher really floundered, despite some significant failings in management. It sounds a little trite, but it was that sense of community that saved my career.

Anonymous, history teacher

In my first few years of teaching, I found student behaviour challenging, as do most beginning teachers. However, a few incidents stood out for me as exceptional and made me question my career. One such incident was at the end of the school day, when two year 7 boys who were packing their belongings up at the end of my class got very angry with each other. In an attempt to diffuse the situation, I asked one boy to leave and the other to stay. But as I walked to stand beside the boy who would be staying, the boy I had asked to leave shoved both of us over. While he didn't physically touch me, he pushed the other boy into me deliberately. He then quickly left, and in order to remain calm, I assured the remaining boy that I was okay.

After referring the incident to my line manager, there was no follow-up. I still work at this school four years on, and I've come to know that some incidents just fall through the cracks. This incident, however, was extremely damaging in terms of the small amount of authority I did have with the student who pushed me. His behaviour intensified, and during the next year he threw various objects at another younger teacher while calling her inappropriate and rude names. Again, follow-up seemed non-existent, but I was in a better position to advocate for this teacher and the boy was suspended.

Other incidents of a similar nature occurred involving some teenage boys who, for reasons of their own, refused to listen to young female teachers. I have had serious thoughts of leaving my career after discussions about these students with some senior leaders that have resulted in comments such as 'maybe he would do better with a male teacher'. This simply is not good enough. I feel like a lack of behaviour support from those in higher positions is very risky for teachers.

Unfortunately, I do believe that without my advocating for the other teacher, no action or little action would have been taken. My school seemed anxious to address these kinds of issues at times, because it indicated a much larger behaviour problem than they were willing to acknowledge. So it was easier to ignore things like this, in the hope that staff would forget about them.

These experiences have been useful in some respects, though, as they have helped develop my teaching and made me realise that rapport is the key to reaching these boys. I get to know them and their struggles – which are usually concerns at home. 'Friendly but firm' is the best advice I was given and can give. Be there for them, but set and stand by firm boundaries. I have also learned to speak up to administration about my worries about students, regardless of whether I'm upsetting anyone.

Anonymous, English teacher
I bumped into some key stage 3 pupils wearing uniform in town once, and after a while, I sensed that they were following me as I walked home weighed down with my shopping and schoolwork. About 100m from my front door, at a secluded spot, one of them threw a full can of coke at the back of my head from a distance of about 5m, though thankfully they missed. It was only as the can passed me that I realised what was happening. I confronted the pupils, who pointed the finger at one another. I couldn't identify the single culprit and ended the exchange, feeling it was futile, with a warning about their conduct whilst still wearing school uniform, only to be aggressively threatened with a physical beating by one of them as he walked away.

When the school investigated, one lad freely admitted everything, only disputing the volume at which he used the threatening language. The school's response seemed good at first. An email from the head said this 'was about as serious as it gets' and the lad who confessed was excluded for ten days. However, no punishment was given to his mates. I specifically asked the investigating SLT member what would happen to the pupil after the exclusion and was told he would be returned to my class and we would 'see what happens'. It made me feel numb and shocked.

I have searched my memory, and although I had previously challenged the lad's behaviour in class, I hadn't given him anything to warrant such a response. I also felt incredibly nervous about having to resume teaching someone who clearly had no sense of right or wrong. What sort of response or behaviour might I trigger in the future from saying something that I felt was innocuous or reasonable?

I feel let down by the school. There were lots of words and 'hope you are okays', but little real, lasting action. I think this is short-sighted, because an attack on one teacher is, fundamentally, an attack on ALL teachers. But the system has let me down too. Schools are under pressure to not permanently exclude, because it looks bad. I have been teaching for way over 5 years, after over 20 years outside education, in both the private and public sector. In no other job would this have been dealt with so lightly, because we cannot 'sack' students.

In my entire teaching career, I have consciously lived as close to my schools as possible, been a 'face' in town and made an effort to be part of the local community beyond the school. My social circle includes parents I met merely through teaching their children. It has made me wonder whether I need to change my career path. One bad apple shouldn't spoil the whole bunch, of course, but I could easily have been seriously injured, yet nothing serious has really happened to deter the student from doing this again. Teaching is the most difficult job I've done. Without proper back-up and protection, I'm not sure how much longer I can do it.

Jane Cross, specialist teacher

I didn't really set out to be a teacher. After four years at art school, a few years of low-paid part-time jobs and being turned down for jobs in the education departments of various museums and art galleries because I 'didn't have teaching experience', I rather reluctantly enrolled on a PGCE.

Much to my surprise, from my first teaching practice I was hooked. I hadn't had a happy experience at school myself and very quickly found myself thinking that being the kind of teacher I would have liked to have had could be quite fulfilling. I was also intrigued very early on at how differently young people could behave in different classes with different teachers, and yet there wasn't wide acknowledgment of this. Usually there seemed to be much more focus on the 'behaviour' of the young person also, rather than a more holistic or systemic analysis of what was happening to cause it.

Teaching art offered more flexibility, perhaps, than teaching a more academic subject (though I did teach A level history of art for a few years), but often students with no real interest in the subject were sent my way because no one was quite sure what else to do with them. I taught in two very different secondary schools for eight years. I was interested in the pastoral side of education and coordinated key stage 4 PSHE (personal, social, health and economic education) too. As it came to the point of making career decisions about which direction to go in, I realised that I was much more interested in this aspect of education than in teaching my subject. I tired a bit of teaching the same things over and over to different faces, but never tired of sorting out problems and trying to win over and motivate more challenging pupils. I had some success with students that others labelled 'difficult' or 'challenging' and so applied for jobs in behaviour support schools.

My first job in this area was in a key stage 4 PRU (pupil referral unit) in an area with high levels of social deprivation. I found this a challenge, as there was a rather 'macho' culture which I found unhelpful for the students and at times unsafe for students and staff. It was a one-year temporary contract and I was not interested in renewing it. I strongly felt that many of the students there would have been much better off in a mainstream setting with the right support, and that the lack of role models and demonstration of other ways of dealing with problems was exacerbating their difficulties rather than helping. At this time, inclusion was the subject of heated debate and I was a strong advocate for it.

I then worked for three different outreach teams as a behaviour support teacher, offering training to school staff and supporting children and young people who were struggling in mainstream schools and often at risk of exclusion. During these years, the heyday of behaviour support services, the exclusion rates fell in many LEAs. Good behaviour support teams made a real difference, and I don't think it is an exaggeration to say they altered the course of lives.

I went on to be an LEA exclusion officer for a few years and then managed a behaviour support team before the public service cuts of 2010/11.

Many teachers cite behaviour as one of the most difficult parts of the job and even consider leaving the profession because of it. Yet for me, it has been what kept me in the profession. I love working with those types of pupils and find achievements with them more satisfying than anything else.

What can I do?

Unfortunately, mastering behaviour management is not a one size fits all, and what works for one teacher in one particular context may not work for another. Furthermore, a school's leadership is vital in creating a positive behaviour culture in a school. As Tom Bennett wrote in his independent review of behaviour in schools (2017), 'how a school was run was an even greater determinant of school behaviour than any one of a number of well-trained staff working in isolation'. But there are certainly strategies and tips that teachers can use, regardless of the support they receive from above, to help them manage behaviour in their classrooms.

Many schools have a clear behaviour policy, which all staff and students are aware of, but as the research has shown, this policy may not be applied consistently. I have worked in schools like this, and it does make it more difficult for all staff to stick to the rules if the rules are continuously bent and reshaped by others. However, it helps if you build a place in your classroom where rules are consistently applied and the students know that you have high standards that are non-negotiable. It is positive discipline. You are not being cruel or unfeeling; you are building a respectful relationship with students, where they know they will receive treatment from you that is totally transparent, as both you and the students are very clear from the outset about what is and isn't acceptable.

Austrian psychiatrist Rudolf Dreikurs believed that what motivated students to behave constructively was a relationship of mutual respect, created by a focus on the consequences of their actions and encouragement from the teacher. Dreikurs believed that there were four main reasons why students misbehaved, and while teachers certainly don't have time to play psychologist alongside the demands of the profession, getting to the root cause of disruption can be a huge advantage in improving behaviour. After all, misbehaviour is a sign that a student is trying to communicate with you, but what they are trying to communicate might not initially be clear. He wrote that students mainly misbehave because they are trying to get attention, because they are exercising their power over others, because they are exacting revenge, or because of fear at displaying an inadequacy (Dreikurs, 1958). I can say from many years of teaching that lots of these reasons still ring true. But how do we deal with this when we are trying to juggle teaching another 30 students at the same time? Using Dreikurs' reasons, we will explore some strategies that could help reach some of your more challenging students.

Attention-seeking behaviours
Of course, it is completely normal for your students to want to get your attention from time to time – it's a fundamental human need. Sometimes, if they don't immediately get the attention they need, this can manifest itself in disruptive behaviour. It is key that we are able to redirect these negative behaviours so that we can help students learn how to get attention in a more positive way. One way might be to give them some attention for behaving in an appropriate way and to catch them doing something brilliant. This positive reinforcement will give them the attention they crave and encourage them to see that there is a better way to get validation than behaving badly.

In some ways, if a teacher reacts negatively to attention-seeking behaviour, this reinforces the message that if the student behaves like that again, they will get attention again. An example of this is when a child shouts out over another child and the teacher then spends a couple of minutes of the lesson time publicly telling the child off: they may find that the child repeats this, as they are getting the attention they want. Instead, focus on the behaviour, not the student. A depersonalised statement like 'I know none of us would shout out over others, as it is rude' gives attention to the negative behaviour, not the child. Then direct your next question to the student who shouted out, so that they can gain your attention for a positive reason. This gives them the tangible reward they were initially seeking and the positive reinforcement to show what is acceptable in your classroom.

Exercising power other others

Some students may feel powerless in the school system, and exhibiting challenging behaviour may make them feel empowered and like they have a sense of control. Sometimes, the teacher can be the scapegoat for this frustration. What makes these students difficult to manage is that the consistent and fair rules approach, which works with the majority of students, may not work here, as a student who does not like authority figures may just see the rules as another thing to oppose. I have come across students like this myself, who no matter how calmly you reason with them, will refuse to back down until you are forced to remove them from your classroom.

With students who show these behaviour traits, I have often found that employing a solutions-focused approach can motivate students to change their behaviour. An example from my own practice involved a year 9 student who constantly behaved in a defiant manner towards me, refusing to complete homework, not attending detentions and completing little work in class. The boy had a teaching assistant who sat next to him in lessons and he hated it, as he felt it brought attention to him. He constantly asked me, probably 20 times a lesson, whether he could move to the back or sit on his own. At first, I refused to let him, as his constant insolent attitude quite reasonably led me to think that he hadn't earned my trust. Yet one day, after reading about the solution-focused approached to behaviour management, I asked him at the end of the lesson what his hopes were for English lessons this year and how I could help him be more successful. He replied that if he could sit on his own, he would do much better. Against my better judgement, I gave him a chance, and six months later, he was a different child. His behaviour changed, as I had empowered him and given him a solution he could work towards rather than focusing on the negative patterns he had fallen into.

Exacting revenge

This is one of the more difficult behaviours to understand and deal with in a student, as it can sometimes be difficult to understand why a student is feeling hurt; they may just be taking it out on the teacher because the teacher is the nearest or most convenient outlet for their hurt and frustration. They could be feeling upset and angry about something that happened between them and their peers, or something that happened at home, or even an altercation with another member of staff at school. Although it is a natural human reaction, the worst thing a teacher can do is take the behaviour personally and react in a vengeful way themselves – easier said than done, I know.

The first step is to try to validate the student's feelings and make a positive connection with them. Dreikurs (1964) said that '[a] child needs encouragement like a plant needs water'. Therefore, trying to find out what the belief of injustice is behind the need for revenge can be helpful in providing the ideas for how the student can be encouraged. Once you know this, a plan can be constructed that will evaporate the revenge cycle in which the student is trapped. Validation statements such as 'Looks like you are having a bad day, want to tell me about it?' or 'I am sensing that you feel XYZ...' will show the student that you care about them and hear their frustrations.

Displacing an inadequacy

Some students struggle with the level of work they are being set in class, and rather than ask for help and appear as if they are 'inadequate' to peers, they prefer to disrupt the lesson so that they can mask their struggles. Aside from differentiation, another important step for teachers to take here is creating a safe and open culture in the classroom, where pupils feel like they can ask for help and reach out without fear of being ridiculed by other pupils in the class.

With this type of behaviour, it is important to focus on teaching learning behaviours alongside the management of the misbehaviour. In order to do this, it's essential that all pupils can access the learning in the lesson. This does not mean that lessons should not be challenging, as this may result in misbehaviour due to disengagement. However, pupils need to be given the opportunity to actively participate in their learning. It is about knowing your pupils and ensuring that if they are not coping with the work, you can offer help before this manifests itself in misconduct.

Changing a learning behaviour is a dynamic process, though, and is not something that can simply be solved overnight. In an Education Endowment Foundation report (2019) about changing learning behaviours, evidence from a conceptual framework adapted from Powell and Tod was used to demonstrate that changing a pupil's emotional behaviour, such as their self-esteem and self-worth, is a dynamic process, with many reciprocal influences, like the pupil's relationship with themselves, with others and with the curriculum.

Figure 14: The behaviour or learning conceptual framework (adapted from Powell and Tod, 2004)

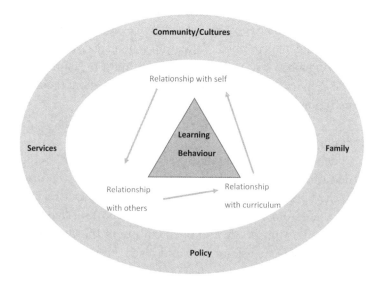

Therefore, to help this student improve their behaviour, there needs to be a three-pronged approach: they need to remember a time when they showed resilience so that they can remember they can do it; the work needs to be accessible and they need to be given praise when they attempt tasks; and they need to know the classroom environment is 'safe' and feel unafraid to get things wrong.

As difficult as it is, it's also important to reflect on our own behaviours in the classroom. We are only human, and I know that there have been situations when I have taken things personally and not used behaviour policies and strategies as consistently as I should have. But the amazing thing about teachers is that we are trained to be self-reflective and will work to improve our relationships with pupils. After all, it really is all about relationships. Reflect on your relationship with your pupils. Is it hindering or helping with your behaviour management? What could you change?

For colleagues in alternative settings such as PRUs, dealing with students who exhibit challenging behaviour traits is their bread and butter. They are experts in their field, and mainstream teachers could learn so much from the strategies they employ. I interviewed two PRU leaders to get some top tips that they thought teachers in traditional school settings could use to improve their practice.

Eleanor Bernardes, head of development and opportunities, Aspire Schools Alternative Provision

Aspire's vision is to support young people, whatever their background and circumstances, to build strong foundations and open new doors. We are led in everything we do by two 'red thread' questions: 'What is best for the child?' and 'How can we make that happen?' We encourage staff to reflect on these questions at all times and to always ask themselves: 'How would I feel if this was my child?' Although we have high expectations in our approach to our curriculum, we are driven to have relationships as a learning goal in their own right.

At Aspire, we enable young people to flourish by supporting them to develop positive behaviours, attitudes and aspirations. We use our behavioural expectations to empower young people to achieve in an atmosphere of safety and mutual respect, where high expectations and the power of relationships are seen as paramount. We aim to remove barriers to learning that may have become entrenched in former educational settings, and we use behavioural expectations to support successful transitions back to mainstream schools, special schools, further education or the world of work. Everyone is expected to behave in a respectful way, to accept responsibility for their behaviour and to encourage others to do the same. We recognise the implicit need for young people to develop the skills that make positive relationship with adults possible.

Everyday strategies for behaviour management

Sometimes you need to press 'the pause button': take a moment to step back and ·think before you jump to conclusions. This will give you time to take a 'helicopter view' and get some perspective. Instead, 'be a detective' and spend some time gathering all of the facts before you come to conclusions and make decisions.

The approach of giving a reminder of how to behave, not giving students a telling off, is always useful, and if that doesn't work, try discussing a student's behaviour with them privately, away from their peers and an audience. That way they do not 'lose face' and do not feel the need to argue. It can be difficult when emotions are high, but never argue; students are good at arguing and having the last word. Allow them the last word as long as they have understood your point. Sometimes, though, you may not get an immediate response, so don't expect one. You need to allow students time to do what you have asked. In the same way, consequences for poor behaviour do not have to be immediate, but students need to know that they will happen. Do not make decisions off the cuff; they need to be discussed where necessary based on the facts.

David Whittaker, Director of Learning, Wellspring Academy Trust

When teachers are worrying about behaviour, what to do about it and how to do 'behaviour management', then they must first think about their own values. Values and relationships underpin every aspect of behaviour management and the key to getting this right lies in your allowing yourself to be your 'true self'.

You need to start with some basic principles that you can use to frame your approach – even if this seems hard.

The concept of unconditional positive regard (developed by psychologist Carl Rogers) gives us all a starting point for working with the most challenging and troubled children. They need to trust adults, not fear them. If we are not careful, we will rely on fear to achieve compliance through the threat of punishment and the generation of anxiety. Rather than generate fear, we must rely on kindness, with high expectations, rigour and support. We can challenge children but support them too. We can have high expectations but with tolerance and empathy. If we understand our pupils and appreciate the challenges they have and the circumstances in which they live, then we can help them rather than fail them. The easy approach to behaviour management is to have strict, non-negotiable rules that lead to no-excuses punishment and ultimately the cliff edge of exclusion. The hard way is to prevent children from being excluded. To do this, we must create a culture where children feel understood. When they feel understood, they will develop self-esteem and then confidence. If children are confident, then they will behave and make an emotional connection to adults. This is the 'buy-in' that teachers need so that they can make learning happen. If a teacher can achieve this, through their skill and determination, then a child will feel loved. Children expect an emotional connection from their teacher, and teachers expect an academic connection from the pupils. We need to aim to achieve both.

Therefore, we must become aware and knowledgeable about where our children come from, what they return to every day and what they have lived through. We must understand the impact of trauma, neglect and poverty on their development and their subsequent responses to stress and anxiety. We must work tirelessly to reduce anxiety rather than add to it. It is vital that teachers in schools understand the basic neuroscience associated with children's behaviour so that we can support and nurture rather than punish and exclude. Behaviour management is never easy. It tests us daily and can be a key factor in us staying in or looking to leave this wonderful profession. However, in order to manage our own anxiety and stress, we must learn to manage the stress of our pupils. We must be calm and resilient without being angry and judgemental. We must be warm and kind, in a way we are with our own children or those close to us. We can provide supportive relationships to children who need them most so that they develop a trust in us, knowing we will not reject them. Children must be allowed to operate in our calm space rather than us being drawn into their chaos.

Behaviour management starts with a basic and clear message – be kind, be thorough, understand the children, develop trust, be tolerant, but have high expectations. You must be true to your values, allow children to have fresh starts, and provide them with the confidence and ability to change and put things right.

Behaviour management is never easy, it just gets easier.

Chapter 5
Reason to leave #5: Toxic leaders

In the last 30 years, schools have changed beyond all recognition from what they were at the beginning of the 1980s. From necessity, they have become more like business organisations and the job of a head teacher can sometimes be so far removed from that of a teacher that a whole new skill set needs to be quickly mastered. Debates have raged in education for years about the employment of non-teaching heads in schools and academies and whether in order to be a successful head you need to have served some time in the classroom first. Of course, it doesn't necessarily follow that a fantastic teacher will make a fantastic head. There is no doubt that a senior leadership position comes with many challenges that go above those a classroom teacher may experience: a huge workload and pressures from both above and below, as well as late-night meetings and constant duties during break and lunchtimes. It's no wonder then, that sometimes leaders make mistakes, and these mistakes can have a negative impact on teachers in the school.

Head teacher Binks Neate-Evans spoke to me about how difficult the role of head teacher can be:

> There are very few decisions you take lightly; most decent leaders will overthink, overstress and underplay their

own good sense of judgement. This is because our hearts are in it. We want to get it right for the children, the staff (all of them, not just teachers), the community and the wider world.

She also told me that because of the immense pressure they can sometimes be under, they don't always do things perfectly:

> It feels great when you are getting it right, but when the opposite happens – a mistake is made or there is disagreement or worse still a critical incident – the burden of responsibility is immense. It's sometimes like being two different people, one almost drowning in empathy, with the other internal voice saying: 'Keep strong. Don't give up. It will pass'.

When we are feeling hurt and overworked, it is sometimes difficult to remember that school leaders are humans, but as Binks states, 'the humanity and wholesomeness of a school can be measured by how mistakes are managed, how you treat people and how you get treated'.

Unfortunately, though, this humanity is not always shown, and in the 2018 investigation into factors affecting teacher retention (DfE, 2018), around one-third of secondary teachers in phase two, particularly those who had been teaching for more than ten years, reported 'a perceived lack of support or trust from the SLT and ineffective school management and policies ... as key contributing factors in their decision to leave' (DfE, 2018: 23). Many of the teachers questioned perceived that they did not feel they were adequately supported by SLTs, particularly with workload and behaviour, and some colleagues felt that SLTs did not listen to their views on or solutions to school issues.

However, many primary and secondary teachers stated that it was the constant accountability and scrutiny they perceived SLTs subjected them to that was driving them out of the profession the most, as they didn't feel like they were trusted as professionals to just get on with their jobs. This can be an extremely stressful situation, but in many cases the increased scrutiny teachers are under could filter down to staff as a result of the increased pressure about school performance that SLTs are subjected to. This scrutiny and lack of trust can be particularly tough on more experienced teachers, who feel that they have proved they can do their jobs without interference and remember a time when there was much less scrutiny. In some cases, the people 'checking up' on experienced teachers have been in the profession for much less time than the member of staff they are scrutinising. This may be a tough pill to swallow.

Some of the teachers questioned felt like the leadership in their school was ineffective and that some senior leaders had forgotten what it is really like in the classroom, so the policies and decisions they made were not fit for purpose and didn't really work at the chalkface. A very small number of teachers, both at primary and secondary school level, felt like they had been bullied by members of their SLT and had been humiliated in front of other colleagues in an attempt to get them to resign or to devalue them in the eyes of other teachers.

Now, I want to make it quite clear that this is not 'SLT bashing'. The majority of senior leaders in school are dedicated, hardworking, caring professionals who work tirelessly to improve student outcomes and inspire the many teachers they work with. Teachers I interviewed told of the amazing support they had received from their school leaders after family bereavement or serious illness, and I am lucky enough myself to work with a fabulously committed and inspiring set of assistant head teachers who are boundlessly positive and encouraging. Senior leaders need to be especially applauded for the difficult decisions they had to make in the light of the COVID-19 pandemic, where, with little warning, they set up new ways of working for pupils and ensured that their schools were open to keep vulnerable pupils safe, all the while taking into consideration the health and well-being of their staff. However, as the research unfortunately shows, some teachers have had experiences with toxic school leaders, which have almost driven them out of the profession they love.

So how would we define toxic leadership? Winn and Dykes (2019) define toxic leaders as those who 'work for themselves or against the goals of their parent organizations, resulting in a poisonous, dysfunctional environment' (Winn and Dykes, 2019: 1). Education consultant Robyn Jackson (Epitropoulos, 2019) believes that there are ten clear signs that a school culture is toxic:

1. No clear sense of purpose or shared common goal
2. Antagonistic relationships between staff, students and parents
3. School rules over mission and purpose
4. Avoidance of difficult conversations with staff and no honest dialogue
5. More self-promotion than collaboration
6. A lack of trust of staff
7. Constant punishment of mistakes and little celebration of achievements
8. People afraid to speak up or have their voices heard
9. Only a dominant few given a voice
10. A fear of taking risks and doing what is right for the students.

If you were nodding your head to any of these, chances are you have worked in a toxic school with ineffective leaders. There are unfortunately leaders and managers who make life difficult for employees in every profession, and sometimes the best thing to do in this situation is to leave and go to another school, where your ideology is more aligned with the senior leaders in that school. However, if you love the school and the students and it is just one senior leader who is spoiling it for you, remember that poor leadership can be short-lived. If you are unhappy, you can bet other staff at the school are unhappy too, and unhappy teachers do not always provide a quality education. Do not despair – they will be found out. Luckily, there are brilliant schools – you do not need to leave teaching. I speak from personal experience.

My story
As a young working-class teacher with tattoos and a visibly alternative appearance, I repeatedly found myself being reprimanded by senior

leaders because of the way I looked. In my training year, at a high-achieving school, I was told that even though my teaching was fantastic, I would never be given a job at the school, because I didn't fit in with their image. The school was run by a former army officer, and the atmosphere was like a military barracks. It wasn't the kind of school I would have wanted to work at anyway, so I didn't let it worry me too much. At my next placement school, they were less worried about the way I looked and more concerned about my accent, letting me know that if I wanted to become an English teacher, I had better 'get elocution lessons', as my strong northern accent wasn't suitable for teaching. After one particular lesson, the head of English screamed at me because I had the audacity to refer to the class as 'guys'. Both of these episodes seriously soured my experience on my placements, and I began to quickly realise that an SLT and management could completely change the culture in a school, in either a positive or a negative way.

In my first school as a proper teacher, I worked with a completely inspirational head who saw my worth and gave me a myriad of opportunities for personal and professional growth. One of the other senior leaders at the school had a reputation for being quite fierce. They seemed to be the ringleader of a clique of favoured staff within the school and would regularly come into lessons and disturb learning to have a joke with a teacher who was their 'mate'. Very early on in my time at the school, I was warned by a more experienced colleague that I shouldn't 'get on the wrong side' of this colleague, because if I did, they would 'get me out'. They then went on to give me examples of former staff members they had forced out of the school, so I was incredibly wary of even speaking to them.

When I became the default head of English, after the proper HoD walked out, I had to work a lot more closely with this colleague. I dreaded every meeting, as they seemed more like altercations. One particular event stands out, when staff were told at short notice that they had to compulsorily attend an evening event. I hadn't had time to organise any childcare, so I let them know that I would be unable to attend because the event was the next day. I received an email back advising me that perhaps I ought to 'be better organised'. My response was quite blunt, and I was immediately summoned to their office and chastised like I was a child.

I spent evenings feeling sick, not being able to sleep because of the thought of having to be in the same room as this person, and one day it all just got too much for me. After being shouted at, I spent my lunch sobbing uncontrollably in my classroom. A colleague intervened and the next morning I was presented with a box of chocolates as an apology. This happened several times. I knew this behaviour wasn't normal, but it was only when I left the school and spoke to other members of staff at the school more candidly that more former colleagues admitted to feeling bullied and victimised by this leader. I only saw them one more time after I left the school. I mentioned that I was doing really well at my new school and was thinking about applying for promotion again. They laughed at me and told me not to bother…very encouraging.

But at the opposite end of the spectrum, I suffered from nine miscarriages before I had my daughter – one of which began at school. Understandably, I was in a hysterical state and one of the assistant heads, whose own wife had been through something similar, took me to the hospital. I didn't know him that well, but he was so kind and gentle, reassuring me in a touching yet non-prying way all the way to the hospital, where my husband then met me. I have never forgotten his kindness. Unfortunately, the loss was not straightforward and was quite prolonged. I tried to return to school a few days later and the head met me at the door and told me to go home for the next few weeks and not to check my emails or set cover. Now that is compassionate leadership.

The difference a positive school culture and positive leadership can make to someone's career is unbelievable. I learned so much from my different experiences about how leaders should behave and feel blessed to currently work with people who treat me with dignity and respect and allow me the professional autonomy to grow as a practitioner. I still haven't ruled out eventually becoming a head teacher myself, but if I do, I will certainly never treat the staff I am lucky enough to work with in a bullying and belittling way.

Voices from the profession

Anonymous, head teacher

I was made a deputy head teacher by an interim head teacher who then left. A permanent head teacher – who would not have chosen me and for whom I would not have chosen to work – was then appointed. He was a misogynist and a bully. Anything I organised or arranged he would double check. If there was anything he didn't like, he would say, in public: 'That's a failure of leadership'. Nothing was ever his fault. He spent most of my line management meetings telling me what he didn't like about me.

Although this was awful at the time, I learned quite a lot from this experience: to keep a record of anything done and said from the beginning, not just when it becomes difficult; don't rant anywhere that is not 100% safe because bullies are fuelled by people, so are terrified they'll be exposed; it's never too soon to leave – don't think, 'Oh, this will look bad' – more and more people understand about bullying than you think. I think it is so important to ensure that you are working for the right people. Lots of kids need you, but you do need to make sure that you stand up for yourself!

I got out to a different school that on paper looked like it would be awful, but which suited me well. I was happy but wanted a new challenge nearer to where my parents lived, and I took a headship that initially went well. In year one I was promoted and in year two I received a £10k pay rise. But then in year three I was pushed out. To be honest, I should have recognised the dangers when the CEO told me he'd cleared out the whole SLT to make way for a new team that I could appoint. I mean, everyone. He was happy when we made the improvements that we had agreed on, but the minute I tried to do anything in a different way, he became very combative. He was also a bully and had people I thought I could trust reporting back on me. He wanted me to treat professionals in a toxic way and I wouldn't. He wanted me to cheat and I wouldn't. In public he was charming, but he was nasty in private, and when I had the chance to leave, I did. I know he later blamed me for everything he didn't like and want, but the biggest message you can take from my experience is not to listen, not to dwell, and to remember what happened accurately. People will always want to tell you things – I just don't listen.

Anonymous, primary school teacher

I should have known from the start that this would not be the leadership team for me. I had alarm bells at the interview – it all sounded too good to be true and the narrative was not focused on teaching and learning. There was a lot of blaming for bad results, which were explicitly attributed to the makeup of the local community. This is something I've never subscribed to. Back in 2002, I was a teacher leading English in a school ranked third bottom in the country; it was bloody hard work, but one of the most joyous experiences of my professional life. I took the position because it was the first advanced skills teacher (AST) job I had seen advertised within commuting distance in over two years of looking. I was desperate. The school community was amazing, but it was a mistake to go against my gut reaction. I have learned my lesson the hard way. Sadly, it was nothing that I didn't already know deep down.

I was so overwhelmed that I couldn't see the simple truths until afterwards. One of the things we were expected to do was to submit our planning for the following week by 4 p.m. on a Friday. I insisted that being this prescriptive didn't help teachers to manage their own workload, and that if we were drawing on assessment for learning to make judgements about future provision, this was nigh on impossible in the timescales being dictated. The head always responded with: 'It's important that teachers have a weekend.' I agreed with her principle. I've never done schoolwork at the weekend; I always start at 7 a.m. and call it a day when I leave the building, which is more than enough. However, I recognised that everyone has different commitments and responsibilities. We also received weekly feedback, which was solely focused on when the planning was submitted (red cross for me, who always pinged over an email as I left the house at 7 a.m. on a Monday morning). We also used to get into trouble for any errors we made in the naming of electronic files – yes, there was even a prescribed 'convention' for this that was apparently very important.

I stubbornly stuck out the position for two years and a term, but I felt like a failure, as I generally like to stay in a school for around five years and I felt truly awful leaving a class at Christmas.

In my next role, I had more empathy but less confidence in myself as a professional, but with the support of the executive head, I was encouraged to spend the year getting to know the school rather than wading in and imposing new systems on the staff. The negative experiences I had gave me a much greater appreciation that we're all in the job for different reasons and that none of these are 'wrong'. I was previously very judgemental about people who were 'just in it for the money', but isn't that why most people go to work? It's not my place to judge others: more to seek out and support them in developing their skill sets and matching these to the needs of the school.

Louise West, head of an SEMH (social, emotional and mental health) school
When you attend any interview, you try to gain a sense of the ethos of the organisation – this goes beyond the website blurb, and in education I've always tried to glean the head teacher's core values during my interview day. It's vital that their beliefs and principles align with yours if you're going to believe in their vision and support their decisions every day. By listening to their opening briefing, talking with students and staff, and observing their relationships with governors and the leadership team, you can pretty much weigh up whether or not you're going to be instinctively loyal and support them wholeheartedly.

About ten years ago, I found myself in my first deputy headship, part of an emerging team opening a new academy amidst opposition from the local community. It was a tough call, and although we were determined to bring together our disparate community and team, the challenge was almost overwhelming; the head for whom I'd chosen to work was pressurised into quick and poorly thought-through decisions that went against her better judgement. After just eight weeks of opening our doors, she was removed, and thus began a stream of various interim leaders.

I had chosen to work for the organisation because I felt inspired by the head's ethos, vision and principles, behind which lay a clear calling to bring opportunity to the less fortunate in society and improve life chances through education. This was, in fact, the vision of the academy chain, but the head I'd chosen to work alongside was driven by humanist values that put people at the centre of everything – a deep sense of caring for health, well-being, family and community that defined outcomes. Get these right first, and then the learning, qualifications, accounts and reports would flow.

Alas, the interim leaders that followed had an array of different agendas and very different ideologies to mine. I watched and learned as the curriculum changed, staff were devalued and parents became disappointed. I had to participate in some of the 'wrongs' because it was my job, including overseeing permanent exclusions, undertaking staff disciplinary procedures, and telling half-truths to stakeholders. I am no idealist; I understand and accept that mainstream school is not right for everyone, that with rights come responsibilities and that accountability is key to growth, but…the half-truths? They made me feel physically sick. I could never understand how wrapping something up in a complex story was deemed more acceptable than just stating the facts. Even a tough decision becomes quite easy to justify if it is simply 'the right thing for the young person'. I found myself at the heart of an environment that felt toxic to me, working for people I just didn't like very much.

Eventually, I found the confidence to follow my moral compass and move on. That sounds quite easy in retrospect, but the move broke my career in mainstream secondary and cost me our family home. Ultimately, I knew that I had kept true to myself and I found strength in that. My family helped me through it and a twist of fate took me into SEN. I went back to classroom teaching, broadened my subject expertise, re-evaluated the things that were important to me and used life's experiences to consolidate my vision of the leader I wanted to be.

Now I'm the head of an SEMH alternative provision and am powered by my values and sense of purpose. I learned so much from watching leaders trying to please everyone yet achieving nothing of any use or beauty – leaders who could make spreadsheets balance but left trails of devastation in their wake. I learned that it's never okay to lie, however much the truth stings, and I now know that it's all right to make mistakes, because people will mostly forgive you if you are honest with them. In fact, they will admire you all the more for being human. I am blessed to still be in education. I try to model the integrity and compassion that was not awarded to me when I needed it and lead the kind of school that I would like to learn in.

Katie Ridgway, lead practitioner English

Going into my NQT year, I was 22 years old. It was March of the PGCE year and I was panic stricken as my classmates somehow managed to find the time to apply and interview for jobs while staying afloat on the course. With hindsight, I should have taken my time. I should have done my research: Google searched, looked at Ofsted reports, read local news, checked out the sheer volume of adverts on *TES* to fill high staff turnover. I have now learned my lesson.

I should have known from the fact that no one came to observe me for the first 15 to 20 minutes of my observation segment of the interview day. I should have known when the head called me to backhandedly offer me the job, despite her saying that they didn't see a great deal of variety in teaching activities (well, you wouldn't after only seeing half the lesson I suppose, would you?) and almost implying that they were doing me a favour in giving me a temporary role. Starting in the July of 2011, at the newly formed academy (two rival schools combined into one), were 13 new members of staff – all bar one of us was an NQT. Another tip-off.

The head was on a mission – to get Good+ in their first Ofsted inspection – and it seemed she didn't care what she had to do to get there.

In that first year, I was shown toxic leadership: staff crying in the staffroom, 'support' plan after 'support' plan which consisted of being observed and berated by the visiting 'consultant' but no actual 'support'. I realise now that there was no actual CPD and no development time to actually support anyone. These plans seemed to be a means to an end.

Countless staff disappeared, off 'sick'. I drove home daily, desperately trying to think of other skills I had so I could pursue alternative career choices. But the truth was, I had wanted to teach since I was about six years old. There was nothing else I wanted to do, but the joy and passion for teaching was being drained from me a unit at a time, if a unit was equal to five lesson plans a day to be uploaded for scrutiny by senior leadership, and there was no agreed time budget, so you felt you had to work every hour under the sun.

I was asked to meet with the head and knew by this point that you didn't meet her without union representation, but mine couldn't make the date 'suggested' by the head's personal assistant, so I asked to rearrange. However, come the date and time of the original meeting posed by the head, she turned up at my classroom door where I was marking. She essentially told me off – how dare I say I couldn't meet with the head and just be sitting marking! She proceeded with her meeting without my requested union representation and informed me that the academy would not be looking to renew my contract next year, to which I responded that the reason I wanted to meet was that I was already going to be handing my notice in.

It was time to look elsewhere. When I got an interview, my head of department told me 'not to get my hopes up'. I'm glad to say I was successful, in spite of her lack of confidence in me.

This experience really allowed me to appreciate supportive leadership when I came across it later in my career. In a recent school, my head approached me (a classroom teacher with no TLR) when the assistant head for teaching and learning post became available. He said that based on conversations we had previously had, he knew it would be a job I would be aiming for at some point in my career. He suggested we go through the job specification and do a gap analysis, from which we concluded that I needed to look at doing the NPQML (National Professional Qualification for Middle Leadership), which he funded in full for me, whether I was to stay at the school or whether it would help me to develop for my next step elsewhere. I had never felt so supported, believed in or capable in the previous five years of my teaching career.

I think my main takeaways for surviving toxic leadership are simple but also difficult to keep in mind when you are in the thick of it. Remember that no teacher is so good or so bad that they cannot improve. Don't listen to anyone who tells you that they have perfected teaching – it's impossible! Equally, there is no '100% perfect fit' school; you may have to make some compromises somewhere. Have the bravery to change your environment – sometimes the grass really is greener. Finally, when you do decide to move on, look for schools where the ethos and values align with yours.

Steph Reddington, former SENCo
Having been at the same school for seven years as a learning support assistant and then an unqualified teacher, it felt like the end of an era leaving. I would have stayed, but turnover was very low, so I was thrilled to secure a job as an NQT at a fantastic, newly built school in a nearby city.

I spent most of the summer setting up my new classroom, making sure everything was perfect, laminating everything in sight and stocking up on new resources. The whole school brimmed with enthusiasm, excitement and promise, which is why it hurt so much to realise that looks can be so deceiving. Very quickly, the reality of the situation became apparent: the head and her deputy had chosen their 'favourites'. I was working for a bully – not just someone who had unrealistic and unfair demands and a lack of empathy or who showed obvious, unprofessional favouritism to her 'chosen ones', but one who was aggressive, spiteful and cruel.

I had a particularly challenging child in my class. He had no formal diagnosis, but it was clear his controlling and violent behaviour arose from an unmet underlying need. I would spend whole afternoons in the corridor with him while he hit, kicked and even bit me. Despite continually requesting support, none came. Instead, after years of 'Outstanding' lesson observations highlighting behaviour management as a strength, my teaching was systematically questioned and undermined.

I remember driving to school and contemplating hitting a tree. I wasn't suicidal, but thought if I did enough damage I wouldn't have to go back for the summer. I wouldn't have to work weeks of 60+ hours, come home bruised, or suffer the toxicity anymore. I didn't hit the tree, but I did decide to hand in my notice and leave the profession. I decided to become an educational psychologist so I could understand and help children like the boy in my class. My resignation was accepted, but not before I was threatened with a poor reference if I changed my mind and applied for a teaching position at another school.

Seven members of staff left that year. Of course, on paper, the reasons were 'legitimate' – some moved, some were promoted, and I was going back to university. Therefore, questions were not asked. One of my biggest regrets is not telling someone at the LEA what was going on, but I didn't know whom to tell and was afraid of repercussions.

Fast forward three years and I'm not an educational psychologist, but having taught in a wonderful special school, I have become SENCo, governor and a member of the SLT in a mainstream primary. Unlike the toxic environment I had previously endured, this new head was the opposite – supportive, understanding, encouraging and motivating. Yes, standards were extremely high, but they were achieved through nurturing and inspiring staff, not through fear or control.

As an SLT, we choose to embed a values-based curriculum, focusing on ethical and emotional intelligence, deepening relationships and building a strong values-based culture throughout the whole school community.

The Latin word *nutrio*, loosely translated, means to nourish, to support, and to foster growth and development. My advice to anybody in a toxic school is to get out. Get out now – you deserve a nourishing rather than a toxic leader, and so your energy would be better spent trying to find one. You don't need to leave the profession; there are fantastic leaders in many other schools.

Anonymous, writer and former teacher

I spent five years working in an inner-city school with toxic leadership. The school was in a very deprived area, which meant it had a number of significant problems anyway, but the leadership, or lack of leadership, exacerbated these. I can see most of the problems only with hindsight, because largely we were worked so hard on a daily basis that I never had time to pause and consider the wider picture.

One of the main problems was that the staff were very young and inexperienced – with the exception of the SLT. Staff turnover was extremely high (it was not unusual for an entire department to have changed over the course of an academic year, for example), because new members of staff were given no support in any way. I mean staff were rarely even shown where the toilet was, never mind talked through what they should be teaching.

SLT members clearly hated each other. I realise now that the head teacher was incompetent, but she dealt with this by playing the members of the SLT off against each other. They bitched about each other in front of other members of staff and would actively look for ways to undermine each other. Largely, they were more interested in petty grudges against each other than in doing their job, and they were unclear of what their job was anyway. This certainly meant they were unable to work together. They were not particularly good. There was no 'strong behaviour person' and, in fact, from a behaviour management perspective, the members of the SLT would generally have been some of the weakest in the school – which is particularly problematic in an inner-city environment. Additionally, their qualifications were often weaker than those of the members of staff they were leading. For example, the head of English did not have an English degree or a secondary PGCE. This meant that he was less qualified than those in his department. In most department meetings and interactions with his department, therefore, he was trying to hide this fact. There was a particularly awkward situation, for example, when he revealed the only Shakespeare he had ever read was *Romeo and Juliet*.

The SLT certainly did not lead by example, and thus we had no confidence that they could. We had a system where they took the top sets in their subject areas on the basis that 'they were the most experienced teachers'. This meant that they avoided the behavioural issues other teachers faced and did not have the C/D borderline pressures or reluctant learners.

The year I left, another head came in following a bad Ofsted. He had a reshuffle of roles and made the SLT reapply for their jobs – then didn't give them to them. They all resigned. Two years later, the school got an 'Outstanding' judgement. However, I can say that I have learned far more from working in that environment than in a school with good leadership, because I now base many of my decisions on doing the opposite of what they would have done.

What can I do?

If you are considering leaving teaching because of a negative experience with a school leader, please reconsider. Remember, one bad apple does not spoil the barrel. For every ineffective manager, there is a committed, wonderful leader who will be a joy to work with – a real leader you want to follow. But if you are currently working with a toxic leader, there are things you can do to try to resolve the issues you are experiencing.

A study conducted in Binghampton University, New York (Spain, Harms & Wood, 2016) identified two types of toxic bosses and how to deal with them: Dark Bosses and Dysfunctional Bosses. Dark Bosses are similar to the leader I spoke about in my own story. They seem to derive a sort of pleasure from damaging and hurting those around them, in a hope that they might elevate their own status and position. The worst thing you can do with this type of leader is to admit that you are afraid of them. They love to exploit the fears and insecurities of others, so the best way you can deal with this is to reframe the criticism they are giving you to make it seem like a positive. If you do this, they will find it very difficult to paint you in a negative light to others, which is something they thrive on. For example, the bullying leader I spoke about earlier knew that I was finding the overnight transition from teacher to leader difficult and exploited this by informing me that the rest of my team were finding my demands on their workload difficult to deal with. I let them win by breaking down and getting upset, which they then reported to other staff members, using this as an example of why I wasn't a great manager. But if I had reframed this, accepting the comment and telling them that I would learn from this, they wouldn't have been able to criticise my response.

However, Dysfunctional Bosses are completely different. They do not want to intentionally harm anybody. They are just not effective leaders, and they have no wish to develop and improve, as they do not see that they need to. It can be incredibly difficult to deal with this type of leader when it impacts on your workload, but try to breathe and think of the bigger picture. Chances are, if you are struggling, others are too, and it can be very helpful to talk to other teachers whom you can trust, so that you see that you are not alone in your frustrations.

Working in a hostile environment can be extremely emotionally taxing. It is important to protect yourself and try to avoid responding in the same negative way, as a negative response will only make the situation worse and send your stress levels spiralling out of control. Try to be as professional as possible and keep a network of others – whom you can trust and to whom you can vent – around you. It is important not to isolate yourself and to have a support base. If the situation carries on, don't be afraid to ask for help. If all avenues have been explored, you are quite within your rights to make a formal complaint to the head or even to the governing body, if it is the head teacher you want to complain about.

Yet if none of this works, it's important to remember that this is only a job and you need to know when to pull the pin. There are thousands of schools out there being run by superb leadership teams who would love to have a committed, experienced teacher like you on their staff. One thing that stood out to me while researching this book is the fantastic experiences and praise that some teachers had for their senior leaders. I have collated some of these below to prove to you that there are schools that will endeavour to deserve you – you just need to find the right one.

Figure 15: Gallery of praise for superb leaders

When I returned to work after being in a coma after having a perforated bowel, my current principal told me 'take your time – we are just glad that you are still alive'. I was anxious and this was such a relief. **@MissPaget**

We got sent mini biscuits, a teabag and a rocky road snack from our head and the PTA this week while we are teaching via remote learning. It was totally unexpected and really thoughtful. **@Hugsutd01**

My line manager regularly tells me to stop working and look after my family. I feel so privileged and it makes me want to work all the more! **@andy_samm**

When they tell you that their door is always open, and you know it's true. When they trust in your work and support your ideas. I got a postcard to say thank you and it stays on my fridge. **@MissCRevision**

My amazing head arranges breakfast for us regularly and puts chocolate in our pigeonholes when she knows we are stressed! **@DCT_Teach**

One member of SLT told my form that it was my birthday, which set off a chain of classes singing happy birthday to me throughout the day. It was very amusing and overwhelmingly kind. **@AnansiRyans**

I am currently taking extended carer's leave while my husband recovers from a stem cell transplant. My head is paying me in full until I return. He said, 'You've been loyal, it's the least we can do'. **@MaisieLuvsBilly**

I was writing a funding bid with my head teacher and deputy head teacher in a Hungarian school. I stood taking notes, summarising and asking questions as we did it. The host school deputy head teacher came in and listened and thought I was the head teacher. My head didn't correct her and afterwards, I asked why. They replied, 'My job is to do whatever I need to let you guys shine.' Amazing human. **@Class_Whisperer**

My head teacher saw on Twitter that I was ill and offered to come and drop off food or medicine if needed. **@LadyGlencora**

Our SLT is human, considerate and kind. That's probably the best summary I could give. **@MrsMoEnglish1**

After I came back from maternity leave, the head asked me what hours and days I wanted to work and wanted to completely accommodate them. No questions asked or snide comments made. **@post16graphics**

It was my first time doing the timetable. On the first day of term, the deputy head came to my office and asked me to come with him. In an empty playground, he said 'Can you hear that?' ... silence ... 'You did that,' he said. 'Everyone is where they are supposed to be, because of you!' **@MsLewis13**

After a lesson observation that couldn't have gone more wrong they said 'That was fun! You coped just fine with all the challenges... that's teaching, you did just fine!' **@caroljallen**

Chapter 6
Reason to leave #6: Bad buildings and no funding

Like many public services, schools are massively underfunded. Sometimes, this can be most evident in school buildings. A study by the Royal Institute of British Architects (RIBA) revealed that one in five teachers has considered leaving their school because of the dilapidated buildings they have to teach in, which are causing them stress and making their jobs much more difficult (the *Independent*, 2016). Under a Labour government, it was recognised that school buildings were not fit for purpose, and £7.6 billion was spent on the 'Building Schools for the Future' scheme, replacing some of Britain's most run-down schools. However, in 2010, this scheme was scrapped by the Conservative government and spending was cut by 60 per cent (the *Independent*, 2016). The poll also revealed that more than 90% of teachers thought that well-built and well-designed schools improved pupils' behaviour and outcomes. The report said: 'The prevalence of damp, leaky classrooms and asbestos-ridden buildings in British schools means too many pupils and teachers are struggling to learn and teach in conditions damaging to their health and education' (RIBA, 2016).

It is a fact that some schools in the UK are simply not equipped for 21st century learning, or, indeed, for 21st century numbers. Some Victorian schools were built to house two or three hundred pupils and are now crammed with two or three times that number. This inevitably leads to congestion at lesson changeovers and unsafe pushing and shoving at social times. It is very frustrating for staff who work in these schools. They do their best in challenging circumstances and build up a resourcefulness that those in new builds don't even have to think about, but on top of an already stressful school day, it's yet another thing to contend with that teachers are tired of.

But this isn't just a few schools. In 2018, *TES* and the ASCL conducted a survey with head teachers which found that more than two-thirds of school buildings in England were not fit for purpose. Almost 90 per cent of them stated that cuts in funding had forced them to scale down or cut some of their routine building maintenance, leading to ASCL General Secretary, Geoff Barton, labelling schools as being in a 'state of national decay' (*TES*, 2018). Some of the problems they identified were leaks, crumbling walls and electrical and heating problems. These issues had resulted in almost half of the heads questioned admitting that they had been forced to close parts of their schools in the last year for the safety of pupils and staff. Perhaps most worrying is the statistic given in the survey that 68 per cent of the schools that took part in the survey admitted they were having problems with asbestos in their buildings. Asbestos, also known as the 'silent killer', has been responsible for the death of more than two hundred teachers in the last ten years (The *Mirror*, 2019). Breathing in asbestos fibres can lead to a cancer that develops in the lining of the lungs, and this can strike years after exposure. Would people working in a modern office building or a bank have to take such considerations into account? I think not. So why should teachers?

Figure 16: Percentage of English local authority secondary schools in deficit from financial year 2010/11 to 2017/18 (Source: Education Policy Institute, 2019)

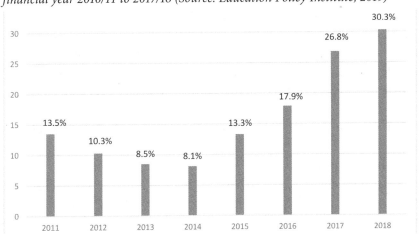

Another consequence of the reduction in funding going to schools is the need for teachers to spend money on buying their own resources and supplies for school. It is clear that schools are teetering precariously on the edge of a financial cliff and teachers are keeping them safe by dipping into their own pockets. A 2019 survey by the NASUWT revealed that one in five teachers spends their own money on buying classroom resources once a week, such as glue sticks, lined paper and pens. To add to this pressure, 45 per cent of those questioned admitted to buying food and clothing for pupils during that year also. The funding crisis is so serious that just before Easter 2018, 7000 teachers in England wrote to parents of the children in their schools informing them that their school was struggling to meet costs (BBC, 2019).

Yet schools have to get their money from somewhere, so some have been forced to ask parents to donate hundreds of pounds a year to pay for essential items like textbooks, stationery and even exercise books. An investigation by *The Times* in 2019 uncovered an example of a state school that was asking parents to donate a whopping £1200 per child each year (*The Times*, 2019). With department budgets frozen and resources desperately needed, there seems to be no other option than for teachers to supplement their classrooms to ensure the students aren't suffering. Essentially, after your basic resources such as highlighters, pencils and pens have been doled out at the start of the academic year, you need to ration them for as long as you can, as you know they will not be replaced. All departments are feeling the strain, but in my own specialism of English, budgets are particularly hard to manage. Every GCSE exam that the students sit is based on books or extracts – all of which the department must meet the cost of. Printing costs alone, to provide the students with extracts to practise exam skills, are astronomical, and that is before you have even started on the key stage 3 curriculum.

With the demands on teachers' workload getting more intense and the pressure from Ofsted to have knowledge-rich curriculums, some colleagues are also spending their own money on paying for SOWs or lesson plans, as they simply don't have the time to produce them themselves. Some of these resources are made by other teachers, which seems like a good way to reward them for their hard work, but companies are also trying to cash in by creating PowerPoints or worksheets that schools can buy in. There should be no need for teachers to do this. Adequate time should be given for them to develop resources and lesson plans during school hours, but we all know that this is not the case.

My story

If I could have a pound for every time I have argued with my husband over the amount of money I am spending on school resources, I would be a rich woman. Every Christmas, I spend hundreds of pounds on chocolate for my classes, a little treat for each child in my form, plus Christmas cards for them. But I don't mind this. It's not a necessity, but it's just something to build relationships and show I care. It's the other things like the glue sticks, the wall staplers and the plastic wallets that irk me. During my PGCE, I had to pay for all of my printing at my placement schools, including worksheets for students to complete during my lessons. I put this down to the fact that I wasn't a proper teacher at the school, but little did I know that this just seems to be a fact of life for teachers in some schools. My experience has taught me that you are just expected to dip your hands in your own pockets and accept that it is part of the job.

I have washed clothing for children whose parents' washing machines was broken, provided sanitary products for girls who couldn't afford them, and regularly bought lunch for those who were hungry. This doesn't make me a saint – I am just an average teacher. There are colleagues all over the country who regularly do the same, though I am truly thankful I am not a primary school teacher, as their need for resourcefulness knows no bounds. While my son was in year 6, his teacher regularly had to provide or source costumes for plays – including a car for *Grease*! However, secondary schools can have just as many difficulties. I once worked in an English department where there were about two useable dictionaries to split between 12 teachers. This led to a member of the department appealing to the local community on social media to donate some if they had them lying about at home. A kind businessman bought 30 dictionaries for each teacher, but this should not have to happen. Imagine a doctor appealing to the public to buy his day-to-day equipment…it just defies belief.

I have also worked in two ancient school buildings – both of which had their challenges. My first school was a beautiful art deco style building from the 1930s. It was a former grammar school in a socio-economically deprived area, with a winding drive and gorgeous wooded land surrounding it. As a vintage enthusiast, I fell in love with it from the first time I walked into the building. The ceilings were high and lofty, with elaborate cornices and stunning light fittings. But the corridor where the English department was located was by far the most gorgeous. It had original polished floorboards and a library with wood panels and a deco style fireplace. The caretakers had looked after it beautifully, but the upkeep on it was horrific and it was on the DfE's 'Building Schools for the Future' list for an upgrade. Like many other schools, it had the rug pulled out from under it through government cuts to the programme. The students were proud of their school and looked after it. I rarely saw any litter and the staff just made the best of what they had, though the

ICT was very temperamental, which meant you really had to think on your feet! The technicians got a workout from the number of times they had to come up and down the stairs to sort out my projector.

The second school I worked in was much larger and part of it dated from the early 1900s, with the other part being a 1950s prefab design. I have never seen a school in such a state of bad repair. It regularly flooded, there were chunks as big as my head falling out of the wall and the corridors were far too cramped for the 1200 pupils on roll. After the holidays one year, I walked in to find my ceiling had caved in all over my classroom floor, but it hardly even fazed me. This school had some of the most committed and superb teachers I have ever worked with, but there is no doubt that working in such a run-down building caused undue stress. Duties were a complete nightmare, as ploughing through cramped corridors meant you were inevitably late to them. Several pregnant colleagues had been unintentionally pushed and shoved by pupils while walking down the stairs, because there just wasn't enough room for everyone to move smoothly between lessons. The head of the school tirelessly campaigned for a new school building, which is thankfully set to open in 2022, so students will finally receive the education they deserve in a building that meets their needs.

This year, I moved classrooms and the teacher who had left the school and used to be in mine had left it in an appalling state. I went in for a couple of days a week all summer to clean, empty and paint it. I spent about £150 on wallpaper, paste, paint and picture frames for it. My husband thought I was crazy, but I am a great believer in the idea that the students will behave in a more respectful way if they are learning in a pleasant space. Besides, I spend more time in my classroom than I do at home during term time, so to me it is important that it is a home from home.

Voices from the profession

Ian Moore, retired principal

Ethos. In my experience, the key to teacher retention is the same whether the buildings are brand new or dilapidated. This key is staff morale, which is first and foremost the responsibility of the school leader. It is their responsibility to ensure that the staff feel respected, valued and supported. When this happens, staff enjoy coming to work and their colleagues become like friends.

The leader makes sure that staff feel welcome to share their problems and ensures they are listened to and given the support they need to help them cope. Staff meetings should be an opportunity to adopt a collaborative approach to curriculum development and pastoral concerns. The leader needs to make time to see staff individually and praise the work they do and be able to make constructive comments as appropriate. In this way, much more than a school is created: a community is created.

Making buildings fit for purpose could be an ideal opportunity for parental involvement. Once parents value the education their children are receiving, they can be asked if any of them could offer their abilities and time to paint sections of the buildings in mood enhancing colours. Of course, the children themselves have a major role to play through displaying their creative and imaginative abilities. Then, even the most run-down of school buildings will become a real reflection of the school's ethos.

But there comes a certain point where the regular dressing up of the dilapidated building has to start winding down. That time comes when there is too much evidence that the building is getting to such a state that it is no longer economically viable to keep maintaining it, or if it is beginning to pose a hazard to health, or if it is simply no longer fit to provide the right environment for children's learning. In order to push home the case, the buildings have to be neglected so that when the appropriate inspectors are invited to visit, they see them as they really are and consequently recommend that a new school is to be planned for. This can obviously be difficult for staff and students who have to teach and learn in these environments.

Yet schools are so much more than a building – even if those buildings are dilapidated.

Kierna Corr, head of nursery

When I first starting teaching at Windmill IPS (Integrated Primary School) in November 2001, I must admit I was daunted by working in mobiles. Even though my then principal had told me that a new school build was on the cards, the contrast between teaching in a purpose-built school and a mobile was still a shock to the system.

But I have to admit that as the weeks went by, I began to see past the stark, grey, flat-roofed buildings that our school was based in and began to make the classroom mine. Mobiles tend to be dark, as they have low ceilings and the windows run along one side of them, but Beverly (the nursery assistant I work with) and I did our best to cheer the space up. I attended an art course shortly after taking up my teaching post and we were encouraged to think about how we displayed artwork in the classroom. I immediately realised that the low ceiling was perfect for hanging artwork from! The fact that you can push drawing pins into any surface in a mobile makes it so easy to put colourful decorations up everywhere. We created display boards on any surface we could; we didn't need designated boards.

My sister-in-law came in one summer and painted a beautiful underwater scene on the walls of the story room. It turned a previously sterile room into something magical. I bought curtains and voiles with nursery rhymes on them to hang at the windows to brighten the place up.

If I'm honest, though, I was delighted to move into our brand new nursery building and school in 2006. I missed the mobile for a while. The ceilings are very high in the new building and I lost all my lovely display space that I was used to, and new buildings are also much smaller than mobile classrooms.

Fourteen years on, I still love walking into the nursery unit every morning, but I have wonderful memories of the drab mobiles too, as it was what was happening inside the buildings that made it all so special, not how they looked. When we all had to walk from our individual mobiles to the staffroom through the playground, I definitely felt more connected to my colleagues and the main school than I do now that I am in a separate building from the main school.

Alexis Doyle, SENCo

Since starting my teaching career over 15 years ago, I have always spent a significant amount on my class and classroom, including resources to use during lessons, craft materials, and creating and furnishing ever-changing role play and reading areas. I have bought PE equipment (balls), provided wet-play boxes, board games, colouring materials and seemingly never-ending craft resources to make Christmas and Mother's Day cards. I have also spent money on spare clothing such as pumps, socks, underwear and spare tights, as well as costumes and props for plays. This has been normalised in schools as 'just what we do', and we are always told there is no available money for any 'extras' once books, pencils, rulers and other stationery items are purchased. I dread to think how much I have spent over the years!

In my SENCo role past and present, I have always bought resources that children with special educational needs require, such as pencil grips, reading rulers, wooden letters and coloured paper – mainly because school budgets are so tight it can take an age to get things authorised, but also because, if I order things myself, I can get next-day delivery and then children have what they need much faster. Professionals such as occupational therapists will recommend special scissors, cutlery, pens, etc., with an expectation that schools will purchase them. I've always wanted to ask, 'Why, if this is a health recommendation, are they not providing them?' Again, I tend to buy these myself. I have also purchased many books and assessment materials and paid for courses out of my own wages to enable me to carry out my job more effectively, and this has run into hundreds of pounds, probably more, over the years.

I teach part-time and my job-share partner and I took over the reception class at the start of the 2019/20 academic year. The classroom was very tired, and we wanted to create a provision based on natural materials and loose parts. We gifted many of the 'plastic' commercially produced toys and sourced natural resources instead. Early years classrooms offer continuous provision, which means that there were roughly ten areas that needed equipping, as well as the outside area. We sourced resources from various places: local online selling pages,

Amazon, eBay, charity shops. We bought cable reels, fruit boxes, wooden blocks, cardboard tubes, wood, corks, shells, wicker baskets... the list was endless.

I personally spent over £500 on setting up the classroom and I know my job-share partner did the same. But the sheer amount of consumables used in an early years classroom is staggering. Children use and lose resources at an unbelievable rate and replacing and topping up the areas with resources is a never-ending job. Add to this the fact that our continuous provision areas need refreshing and new enhancements added every two weeks, and it's a massive additional cost. As an example, I wanted my class to make Easter nests recently. The materials to make these cost me over £20 and that was just for an activity that took an afternoon. If I calculate how much I spend on average each month either on Amazon, eBay or just when doing my weekly shopping, it is over £100, sometimes more. We shouldn't have to do this, but if we don't, then our provision would not be as enticing, and we want children to have the resources they need to make the best possible progress. It's an expensive job, this teaching malarkey!

Tips I've learned along the way are to re-use and recycle materials. As an early years teacher, you start to see things in a new light! Empty bean tins become pencil pots, boxes for the recycling become materials for junk modelling, and before anything gets thrown away at home, it is given careful consideration! I have also become very good at asking for things: family members have donated shoes, hats, handbags and costume jewellery for our role play area; staff members donated old pots and pans for our mud kitchen; I have put umpteen requests on local online market places for donations of materials and resources. We also make some of our own resources, such as play dough, mini books for writing in and maths board games. Of course, making these things also takes additional time, usually at the weekend, which eats into our precious family time.

This year, my school asked parents for a termly donation of £5 from each child to give teachers a fund from which to buy consumables, but this has not proven very fruitful. The first term we had £55 in donations, but by last term (admittedly straight after Christmas), we only had £25 in donations. It was good idea, but once again it is mainly teachers propping up the dire funding in our schools.

Gemma Campbell, FE (further education) lecturer and teaching and learning mentor

When I was offered a job as head of faculty 300 miles away on the edges of Northumberland, my colleagues warned me of extreme weather: the snow, the cold, the interminable darkness. I didn't believe them. My biggest concern, I thought, was creating an English department almost from scratch. The department was hosted in two previously condemned 1970s portacabins from the old prep school. These were on the edge of the school grounds, next to the woods that led to the walled garden. The classrooms were tatty at best, with single-pane aluminium windows, temperamental electric heaters and neither a book nor a hint of technology evident. However, the outside space spoke of being a great stimulus for descriptive writing lessons, and I envisaged summers spent learning outdoors. I was promised a brand new department building incorporating a new drama classroom, learning support team rooms, and the English classrooms, and I fully believed the promise. This school was investing and on the up. Plus, my budget was almost a blank cheque to attempt to create an inspiring department, ready for the much-anticipated inspection that was due.

By the time the students arrived in September, the insides of the shabby portacabins were freshly painted, with bookshelves and some new gravel scattered around the muddy entrance outside. Each classroom now had a portable projector and two new wall heaters. My colleague and I had also created bright displays with a POETREE, washing-line words strung across the ceiling and what we thought was a really interesting and broad curriculum, all supported by brand new texts and a few classics too. Then came the November and December snows, which forced us to become more of a travelling show, trying to find available rooms in the main school. For much of that winter, the classrooms were inaccessible because of the snow drifts and being bloody freezing, even with our extra electric heaters.

By the March of that academic year, as the inspectors arrived, we had a veritable library of books, from the Oxford Shakespeare collection to my favourite dictionary dinosaurs – 2 in 1 dictionary and thesaurus. We had textbooks for all of key stage 3 that were aligned to the National Curriculum, and our key stage 4 texts were brand new, as it was the big GCSE year of change. We worked closely with the beautiful school library, hosting one lesson a week for our key stage 3 students just to get them out of the freezing portacabins. We also had one lesson a week for all years in the ICT rooms for the same reason, and when the report was published singing our praises, I fully expected the summons to the headmaster's study to discuss the new classrooms and have a design meeting.

But unfortunately, my colleague and I had done so well decorating, revamping and delivering our subject in the previously condemned cabins that they decided to reallocate the funds to moving the home economics department to within the main school buildings, as suggested by the inspection report. Realising that success was, in fact, not the way to a new building or even a relocation into the main school building, I finished my next year and tendered my resignation after what seemed like two very long dark years. I'd achieved as much I was going to be able to and it was time for pastures new – somewhere warmer, lighter and closer to friends and family.

Julia Coles, deputy head

With just over 110 pupils, our successful primary special school had outgrown our site, which had only ever been intended for 80 pupils. We'd filled every nook and cranny and even turned the staffroom into an additional classroom! We had a wide catchment area encompassing several East Midland towns, and many of our pupils had long taxi journeys at the start and end of the school day.

We had a large staff team and staff had nowhere to congregate together, unless it was a whole school meeting held in the hall. Staff took their breaks in the local park or sat in their cars to eat their lunch. There was nowhere to do PPA or hold meetings.

Discussions with the LEA ensued – we knew our school roll was rising and we were open to various suggestions. Finally, a solution was proposed that worked for everybody. An old Victorian infant school stood vacant in a nearby town (6 or 8 miles away, depending on which route you took). It would need lots of refurbishment but could provide a second site, thereby reducing demand on the current site and enabling some children to attend a school in their local area – similar to the school experience of their mainstream peers! The old site would have capacity for 100 children and the new site would have capacity for 56. We would remain as one school, one DfE number, one inspection, but two sites! The plan was that we could take three years to gradually fill our two sites from a roll of 132 in order to reach our capacity of 156!

Architects were appointed and plans were drawn up – this was our chance to create our vision. But dreams had to be tempered by reality. Issues with damp, flooring, and bats in the roof space all ended up taking huge chunks out of the budget. Deadlines moved, with the opening date seeming to move further and further away. Finally, an Easter opening was agreed. Still problems arose. 'Let the tradesmen get on with their work and we will give you the keys just before Easter' instead became 'We will give you the keys on the first day of term!'

An additional training day for staff enabled all hands on deck, and in just one day, boxes were unpacked, shelves were filled and posters put on the walls. A day later, in April 2015, 29 children arrived in their new school, some moving from the previous site to be closer to home and others arriving for their very first day in a new school.

The old site had its staffroom refurbished, with new furniture bought so that staffrooms on both sites offered the same experiences to the staff team. Finally, staff had a place to call their own at break time!

Increased space in classrooms led to improvements in pupil well-being and behaviour, and this in turn seemed to impact positively on the well-being of staff.

As a school with two sites, we have had to work harder to ensure consistency across both. New staff are appointed to 'the whole school' and then allocated to one or other site, with a fair share of new and experienced staff spread across each site. Resources are shared across both sites and there are basic stocks of certain items on each site. Children and staff visit both sites for events and activities. It is all totally collaborative.

Capacity has continued to grow, with the LEA increasing demand for places. In April 2020, we had 189 pupils on roll across the two sites, and guess what we are looking for? You guessed it…another site!

Allen Tsui, primary school teacher

Long before concerns about how schools removed from LEA control would continue to observe the annual recommendations of the School Teachers Pay and Conditions Document, one of the peculiarities that perplexed staff working in London schools was the supplementary allowance known as 'London weighting'. Retained from a bygone era of the civil service, it allows public service organisations including schools the ability to 'enhance' annual salaries from the national scales for schools in England, with current amounts varying from just under £1200 to over £9000 for somebody who is on the maximum of the upper pay range. The justification for this local pay allowance has been higher costs of living in London and staff retention.

Can such justifications still apply? Based on data produced by HM Land Registry, the 'average' purchase price of properties in April 2020 in London, even for the smallest dwellings, were in excess of £0.5 million or an astonishing 16 times that of an NQT's pay rate, even for one of the 'Inner London' schools. As a life-long Londoner who entered teaching as a second career, it breaks my heart to think that neither my primary-aged children nor my colleagues will be able to afford to own their own property neighbouring mine. The Victorian dwellings that were originally built for the 'working classes' across so much of London have, since the 1990s, become the brick bastions of those who can rely on the 'Bank of Mum and Dad' or who are literally fortunate enough to work in mega-salaried jobs in, for example, international finance. A quick online search of properties for rent suggests starting costs of £1000 per calendar month for a one-bedroom flat – which again would equate to about two-thirds of an NQT's monthly net income. Whilst it might be possible to rent more cheaply in a house share, such arrangements often bring other issues to the fore.

As for staff retention, this is a little trickier to explain. London is a magnet for people who have trained and worked in places such as Canada and New Zealand as well as other countries where teacher training programmes and the school systems are highly valued compared to England. It is therefore entirely possible for any school needing to address an immediate staff shortage to quickly recruit, especially given the plethora of supply agencies that 'feed' the 'system'.

For those like me, who are life-long Londoners, the decision to be a teacher in London and whether or not to secure a permanent position in a school that pays the maximum amount in London weighting is a tricky one. Since I qualified as a teacher in 2012, I've always worked in schools that are categorised as 'Outer London'. I have been fortunate enough to spend most of my time as a teacher so far working in an 'Outstanding' school where the leadership is amazing. Both the learning opportunities for the families who attend the school I work for and the support for staff development would be hard for any school to match, even in the independent sector. It is, however, one of the struggles in the staffroom to hear how colleagues have joined and left because the 'cost' of working in an 'Outstanding' Outer London school could be as much as £2000 per year when travel time and fares or petrol money are taken into account. Such an anomaly is further exacerbated when there are some schools less than a street apart but across a borough boundary, where one side of the zebra crossing pays the enhanced rate but the other does not. It might not sound like very much money, but occasionally it may make the difference between some teachers who are really struggling to make ends meet being able to afford a meal or not.

What can I do?

The easiest way to stop spending your own money on classroom resources is to just refuse to buy things. It may seem like you are doing something fantastic and doing it for the kids, but you're not, and if you continue to keep buying basic things that your students need to complete their learning, this will just continue and things will never change. Departments cannot run forever on goodwill alone, and the government should surely be funding schools properly so that this doesn't have to be the norm. If you think about it, it is the equivalent of a police officer buying their own uniform or handcuffs – which of course sounds completely ridiculous.

However, if you feel you must spend money on things to help your teaching, there are ways that you can reduce this and spend smart. But what kinds of supplies are teachers spending their own hard-earned wages on? In the UK, there hasn't been much research on this. However, in the US, there also seems to be a problem with teachers spending huge chunks of their wages on classroom supplies, and a lot of work has been done there to research what kinds of things they are buying. The diagram below illustrates this, and these items probably bear a striking resemblance to the kind of resources UK teachers are also splurging on.

Figure 17: Top 5 classroom supplies teachers buy with their own money in the US (Source: Adoptaclassroom.org, 2019)

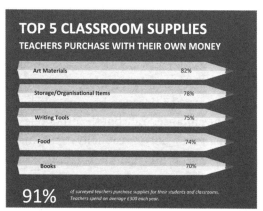

Firstly, the 'writing tools' come as no surprise. If you are anything like me, your classes will seem to go through pens like nothing you have ever seen. I can buy a box at the start of the week and then, by Friday, around half haven't been returned. To counteract this, I've bought baskets for the centre of all my tables, with highlighters, pens, pencils, sharpeners and everything else that students need to complete their work in the English classroom. Although this was an initial expenditure, we are now two terms in, and the baskets and their contents are still intact. This has taken quite a lot of training with pupils, who need to count what is in the baskets while standing behind their chairs at the end of the lesson, waiting to be dismissed. This could even be given as a job to students who are crying out for a position of responsibility in the class, where they could be rewarded with credits or achievement points at the end of the term for making sure people take care of the baskets. It might also help to use current affairs to help you remind pupils about not damaging and losing equipment. Many students have seen the Attenborough documentary on the BBC about plastics polluting the ocean and have done lessons in school following up on its key messages. If you remind them that pens and highlighters are made of plastic and that we ought to be using as little plastic as we can, this might drive the message home.

Now I don't know what it is with glue, but students seem to eat it, it disappears that quickly. They often spread it on the back of their worksheets like butter on a piece of bread, so no sooner have you bought it than it's gone. Rather than putting the glue into the box with the rest of the supplies, I now circulate the room and put four dots on the corners of the worksheets myself, so I can stick it on. I know I seem a bit Scrooge-like, but my finances are much healthier.

When it comes to exercise books, there is absolutely no excuse for schools not having provisions for students to write on. Buying textbooks and key texts for lessons, though, can be a hefty expense. There are thousands of schools up and down the country that have books sitting languishing in stock cupboards and discarded in the corners of classrooms. Many are now selling their stock at really cheap prices online in a bid to raise some cash and free up some space. There are also subject-specific teacher groups on social media sites such as Facebook, where there are regular posts from teachers who are looking to swap or give away class sets of books, and this is a really excellent way to build up your texts for free or very cheap.

If you are a form teacher, paying for treats at Easter, Christmas and end of term can soon add up. As an NQT, I made individual presents for each student in my year 11 class and year 11 form. Not only was it expensive, but it took hours! Did they appreciate it? Sure, they seemed to at the time. However, I have since learned that they would have appreciated a couple of packs of cheap biscuits and bottles of juice just as much. Baking simple fairy cakes or cookies can be much cheaper than buying chocolate, and you can make them look really fancy with a bit of cellophane, ribbon and imagination. Scouring pound shops and buying multipacks of lollipops is also a much cheaper option. Perhaps the best presents I have given my form are personalised cards and letters, though, which cost nothing and really show you care. I bumped into a parent of a challenging boy I taught a few years ago, who was now in his 20s, and she told me that the letter I wrote him when he left school is still on his wall. It made me all warm and fuzzy inside and just demonstrated that showing you care doesn't have to cost anything.

As we have read, working in a school with a building that is dilapidated and run down can be tough. However, there are small changes you can make to your classroom to make it into a little oasis of learning and calm. If you have any spare paint at home and your school agrees, even painting one wall in a brighter colour will hide the state of disrepair of the rest of the walls. Displays are also a great way to bring a bit of cheer into a great classroom. Apps like Pinterest are full of inspiration for innovative displays you can copy or adapt. Things like 'working walls', where students can pick up sheets or past papers are excellent, and I also like to ensure that my displays promote issues such as lesbian, gay, bisexual, transgender and questioning (LGBTQ) rights or showcase Black, Asian and minority ethnic (BAME) writers, as it's so important to educate students about these issues as part of their learning. A quick morning using a search engine will also throw up many educational companies or charities who will send schools free posters to use on their walls or on displays.

Finally, although working in an old building has its challenges, there are millions of schools around the world who have it much worse.

A teacher on Twitter told me that when she worked in a school in Ethiopia, they only had electricity every few days. For another book, I interviewed educators who have taught in concentration camps and in war zones. Although this may not help alleviate your current situation, it is good to sometimes have a bit of perspective. Teachers are incredible and their commitment means they will make the best of any situation. If the students love the school and you create an engaging learning environment which they respect, the surroundings really don't matter.

Chapter 7
Reason to leave #7: Where is my autonomy?

Teachers are committed, dedicated professionals who do a truly vital job. Every day, parents trust them with their most precious things – their children. Often, a teacher has an enormous influence on the developing mind of a child. Many would therefore agree that it is only right and proper that there should be some level of legislation and scrutiny in the job. However, the lack of autonomy in schools is frequently cited as a reason why teachers are choosing to leave the classroom as they struggle to cope with the perceived lack of trust in their ability to do their job. In the 2018 investigation of factors affecting teacher retention, educators felt they needed fewer constraints and policies dictating how they should teach their students so that they could teach in a way that was best suited to their own pupils (DfE, 2018). Teachers spoke about feeling stifled by the lack of creativity they had and said that the only way to retain teachers was by having fewer policies, a focus on achievement, and a more child-centred approach. The excessive evidencing constantly required across both primary and secondary education is turning teachers into box tickers and eroding their confidence and self-efficacy.

Psychologist Albert Bandura was one of the first scientists to explore the concept of self-efficacy, defining it as our own judgement of 'how well one can execute courses of action required to deal with prospective situations' (Bandura, 1982). His self-concept theory goes some way to explaining why teachers may be feeling a lack of confidence, as he argues that how we perceive our own abilities is based on clues we receive from external sources. This self-concept is dynamic and ever changing, so if teachers find themselves constantly scrutinised and checked up on, they will believe that they are not up to doing the job. If you begin to feel incompetent and not trusted to do what you were employed to do, this will lead to low self-efficacy and, before long, a belief that you are incapable of the work and perhaps should not be doing it. People with a high self-efficacy will generally feel they have more control over what they do in their working lives, whereas those with a lower self-efficacy feel that their hands are tied and that what they do at work is completely out of their control. These feelings can have a huge impact on both teachers' motivation and self-belief. Eventually, if a classroom practitioner loses their self-confidence and motivation to do the job, this could lead to work-related stress.

Figure 18: Correlation between self-efficacy and self-belief (Source: Bandura, 1982)

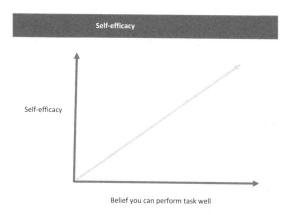

In a study by Michie in 2002, it was revealed that the organisational culture of a workplace can be a huge indicator in work-related stress and that a perceived lack of control over work and lack of participation in decision-making can be a trigger. It's not really difficult to see how this might become the case. If teachers continuously have their every decision predetermined, their creativity completely stripped, and each thing they do scrutinised under a magnifying glass, the job can soon become monotonous and soul destroying. In the *Guardian*'s 'Secret Teacher' column (2013), a primary school teacher wrote about his frustration with having to stick to a preconceived script of reading and curriculum choices, saying:

> So this is how my vivid, varied days became monotone and dull. My exciting lessons full of enthusiastic learners have become formulaic sessions where I go through the motions, and the children, to their credit, continue to work hard to learn.

It is a frustration so many other teachers up and down the country share.

The picture is clear: teacher autonomy is associated with higher job satisfaction and intention to stay in teaching (NFER, 2020). This also correlates with the responses I received from the qualitative research I conducted across the UK. Teachers were tired of having to constantly teach the same lessons on the same days to their classes and not being able to stop and go over concepts the students hadn't grasped, for fear of being reprimanded for deviating from the plan. Teachers were tired of constant drop-ins and work scrutiny. One teacher told me that they had six members of the SLT drop in during a single hour-long lesson! They said that the students had even commented on how ridiculous it was. Teachers are tired of the fact that their professional judgement doesn't seem to count for much and that instead there is an over reliance on evidence and data, where even current working grades given at assessment windows need to be justified to your line manager.

It is simple psychology. Self-determination theory dictates that we are motivated by both intrinsic and extrinsic forces that drive us to behave in certain ways. These external forces can include observations at work, marking scrutiny, the respect and admiration of colleagues and the freedom to make your own professional decisions.

According to Deci and Ryan, extrinsic motivation is a drive to behave in certain ways based on external sources and resulting in external rewards (1985). Such sources include grading systems, employee evaluations, awards and accolades, and the respect and admiration of others. Intrinsic motivation comes from within, from our own morals, values and interests. These two motivations are not diametrically opposed, yet they do lead to two different types of motivation: the autonomous motivation where we want to do something, or the controlled motivation where we are forced (Ryan and Deci, 2000). Clearly, being constantly forced to behave in a certain way or teach in a certain style may result in us not really taking our brain to work and just going through the motions instead. When a teacher is intrinsically motivated and allowed to teach in a way that aligns with their own interests and ideology, they are much more self-directed, resulting in more enjoyment and satisfaction in their career. When a teacher is non-self-determined at school, they become unmotivated, have no personal attachment to their job and feel a lack of self-control.

Figure 19: The Self-determination continuum (Source: Ryan and Deci, 2000)

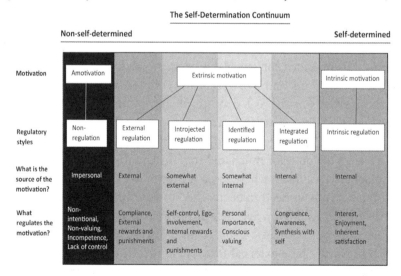

(Based on Ryan, R. M. & Deci, E. L. (2000) 'Self-Determination Theory and the Facilitation of Intrinsic Motivation, Social Development and Well-Being', *American Psychologist*, 55(1), pp. 68–78)

Increasingly, dedicated teachers are choosing to change careers, as they can no longer cope with the intrusion. For experienced teachers, the scrutiny and micromanagement may seem even worse, as even only ten years ago it seemed that teachers were allowed a lot more creativity to deliver the core curriculum content in the way they thought best. The job has changed dramatically even in the time I have been teaching. Of course, as the beginning of this chapter stated, it is important that teaching is regulated, as there needs to be some level of quality assurance. However, teachers also need to be given some level of autonomy to feel they are trusted and valued in their schools. I have experienced both extremes and I am sure many of you can relate to my experiences.

My story

As you've learned, I came into teaching later than some, having spent some years in the stressful world of national newspaper journalism. It's fair to say I was a little cocky; I didn't think I was like other NQTs and that I really needed to listen to people, as I knew what I was doing. Big mistake. The HoD saw the potential in me, but also knew that I needed some guidance to keep me on the straight and narrow. As a journalist, I had been largely used to managing myself in terms of my working day. I certainly wasn't used to being micromanaged and having my professional judgement questioned, and it wasn't long before I was in trouble.

On one particular occasion, the head asked me to help lead an event and I forgot to tell the HoD. She quickly had me in her office when she found out and told me that from now on anything that anybody asked me to do had to go through her before I agreed. I was quite shocked by this, but thought it must just be the way teaching is, so agreed and apologised. Although she liked to be in control, this middle leader went on to be the best I ever worked with. She struck a superb balance between guidance and support and professional autonomy. For example, we had schemes of learning and lesson resources that we could all use, but so long as we covered the key skills, she was fine with us delivering the content in whichever way we saw fit. Importantly, she embraced personality in her teachers and never had any wish to dampen us down and turn us into robots.

However, when you become a school leader, it gives you an entirely different school experience. When you are in the classroom, it can sometimes feel that middle and senior leaders are unnecessarily spying on you – checking up on you for some kind of ego trip. But once you are in that position yourself and see the immense pressure that leaders are themselves under, it is much easier to be sympathetic when it sometimes inevitably cascades down. Being a curriculum leader in a 'Special Measures' school is like no other pressure I have ever experienced. It felt like there was an octopus on my back. Each of its slimy tentacles was a meeting I had to attend or a check I had to do on the members of my team, and it was as though it was trying desperately to pull me down into the abyss. It was almost impossible to stay afloat. Try as hard as I might, I couldn't manage it all by myself, and to my shame, I ended up piling pressure on my team. I would do so much of what I did back then differently now, and would have much more confidence and belief in my own ability to question what I was being asked to do and how it benefited the students. When I decided to step down from this position, I wanted complete autonomy. I felt so depressed, like I was trapped inside a cocoon. I decided that I needed to find a school where I could break out and unfurl and spread my wings.

Yet I have also experienced teaching in a school where things are too laissez-faire, where teachers are left to just do what they like and there are no policies or scrutiny and little quality assurance. Rather than the utopian dream this may seem to be, it can result in chaos. Unfortunately, in any walk of life, there will be those who choose to take advantage of a situation like this, do the bare minimum and shirk their responsibilities. Luckily, these people are few and far between in teaching, but there definitely needs to be a balance somewhere between the two extremes.

I am lucky enough to have found somewhere that allows me to fly and show my creativity and individuality as a teacher, while also providing me with a structure I can refer to and follow. So many teachers have been through experiences like mine and know that being constantly under the microscope can feel intrusive and demoralising. However, many have found ways of remaining positive and breaking out of these bonds.

Voices from the profession

Anonymous, teacher of English

At a previous school, the lack of autonomy was a gradual, insidious process. We had a large number of supply teachers, so it began with the demand that all SOWs had to be accompanied by step-by-step lessons, done in PowerPoint, so that there would be consistency across the department and no pupil would 'suffer' from being in a class led by supply. This continued for a month or so. Then lesson observations began. Lessons and their organisation were criticised for not being identical, and the SLT claimed that we were failing our classes by not following 'the script'. Protests about being unable to differentiate or adapt to suit the needs of our classes had us labelled as a maverick or as not being a team player.

Then the book trawls began. We were now not only expected to teach identically, but we had to mark identically. Every piece had to have a wow/how/now response. What was 'wow' and 'how' could it be improved? The 'now' involved a task that the pupil had to do to address this. The next step was green penwork from the pupils before the work was re-marked by us. The workload became onerous. Pupils began to get stressed, as planning wasn't catering to their needs.

The lesson observations continued but became more critical, with any negatives picked out and very little focus on positives. Self-doubt began to creep in. We stopped getting individual feedback and got general feedback in department meetings instead. It was brutal.

Self-doubt made way for a complete lack of confidence. I had been teaching 25 years by this time and began to wonder if I could continue to teach.

Pupil behaviour deteriorated and positive teacher–pupil relationships were affected. Pupils' marks began to go down and I began to run extra classes after school because I was concerned about the fallout…for both them and me. An external 'advisor' was brought in, who advised tightening up the observations and having more book trawls. In the first term of her arrival, three English teachers left. By the end of the year, I and three others had gone too.

I had been persuaded to apply for an English teacher job in another local school. My experience here was totally different. There were clear SOWs, but how I chose to teach them was up to me. To be honest, I spent the first term waiting to be criticised, but the criticism didn't come. I was thanked, appreciated and trusted. The head would often pop in to see me and tell the pupils how lucky they were to have me. Book trawls were about sharing good practice rather than finding fault, and lesson observations were not graded. Now we do triads, where we are encouraged to take risks while being coached by colleagues. My results have gone from strength to strength and I have my teaching mojo back. I have had a promotion, and my 30-year experience is valued inside and outside of the classroom. I love my school.

We recently had two jobs come up as a result of internal promotion, and we were inundated with applicants. The biggest draw? Autonomy! Too many of the applicants were working for schools who were stifling them, and they had had enough.

Mr Millinchip, primary teacher

My first teaching role, as an NQT, was in a small independent school with one class teacher per year group. I was given a mentor and a lot of global support, but on the whole, I was left to be autonomous with my class. It felt like a dream start; I could do what I wanted with my first class.

The truth of the matter is, it wasn't as perfect as it sounds. The school remained a friendly environment, but that autonomy turned into a combination of apathy and laziness. I am sometimes guilty of being a coaster, and this freedom played to that side of my personality: I could do the bare minimum and get away with it. The older me would have chided the younger me and said that this was a golden opportunity to experiment. Sadly, I wasn't at that point in my development. I needed guidance from the experts around me and I ended up feeling a bit lost. It all hit home when I had a meeting with a difficult parent who asked me a lot of probing questions. I realised I couldn't confidently reply with sound advice and concrete answers, and I am usually quite good at spin. I had been shown up.

When I moved, I joined a school with a strong reputation and historically excellent inspection reports. The school was due an inspection and it was all hands on deck to maintain the reputation. It wasn't, however, one of these strict authoritarian schools. The head was a suit-wearing inspector but was generally calm and supportive, treating colleagues as the experts they were, not as his minions. In terms of autonomy, I still felt I could do a lot of what I wanted, but the parameters were made clear from the start. You could explore the innovative side of your role and could collaborate regularly with others, but you still had to stick to a quality assurance timetable and contribute to the wider school when required. The school was a fantastic family and was always looking forward. It didn't forget its foundations and the fundamentals of teaching.

The school I am in now is only three years into its journey and I came hoping to share my expertise. I feel that I now have the knowledge and confidence to help the school move forward. This wouldn't be possible if I hadn't been given my autonomy with guidelines early on and the opportunity to work with high calibre teachers.

Teachers are highly skilled and hugely creative, but we are still creatures of habit. If it is done in the right way, a rigid framework in a school – combined with teaching autonomy and trust in the expertise of each teacher – will produce some exceptional results.

Nathan Douglas, deputy head teacher

I believe that teacher autonomy is extremely important within the teaching profession. In my experience, high levels of teacher autonomy, when underpinned by rigour, have many advantages, including, but not limited to:

- high teacher perceptions of self-efficacy (leading to motivation, self-esteem, betterment of practice and, ultimately, retention)
- creative lessons that foster challenging and purposeful learning
- meaningful and purposeful links being made across the curriculum
- better outcomes for pupils from a broad and balanced curriculum that stimulates, enthuses, engages and excites.

I am not advocating that class teachers should be given the National Curriculum and just let run with it – although, depending on school and teacher workforce, this could work in theory! My philosophy for teaching and learning is based on 'Rigorous Autonomy'. This, I believe, is the fine balance between two interpretations of how the National Curriculum should be implemented:

Figure 20: Rigorous autonomy

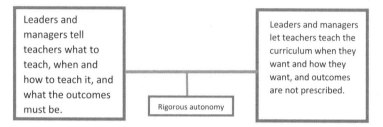

I have worked in schools at either end of this continuum, and I truly believe that rigorous autonomy is the best practice. This is where leaders and managers lead and manage their subjects and areas of responsibility with the rest of the teaching staff. Changes are discussed, debated and thought through with the staff, so that everyone is a part of this process.

Subjects are organised into carefully thought-out knowledge, concepts and skills, with no direct prescription of when to teach, how to teach and what the outcomes must be (apart from the fact that outcomes must be high quality). Cross-curricular organisation is encouraged and fostered. There are no formal weekly planning trawls; instead, planning is checked on a half termly basis before the next set of teaching begins, and helpful, kind and specific feedforward is given to check that the rigour of the subject is upheld.

Learning walks or lesson observations do not take place; instead, coaching lesson visits followed up with time to discuss lesson rationale and pedagogy are given. Crucially, this is not in the form of feedback. Rather, it is a mutually derived feedforward that nurtures rigour within teaching practice.

Less experienced subject leaders are also coached on how to lead and manage their areas of responsibility. This coaching empowers the new leader to take more and more ownership of their own subjects and they are encouraged to impart their own rigorous vision on the subject.

In summary, rigorous autonomy is not only a philosophy; it is an ethos that must begin with the SLT, cascade to the middle managers, and, through a process and journey, be embraced/bought into by the rest of the teaching staff. Otherwise it won't work. Rigorous autonomy is a journey to a great curriculum, great teaching and great outcomes for all.

Anonymous, English teacher

I have worked in both an autonomous environment and a highly controlled environment. Having worked in both, I think somewhere in the middle is the healthiest place to be, but I would also argue that the question of autonomy is quite context dependent.

The highly controlled environment was of my own doing, as I was the head of department. I look back and sometimes reflect that I was too controlling, but I am also very conscious of the position we were in. When I joined my last school, it was in a really bad way, and within six months the head had been released. We barely scraped a 'Requires Improvement', and standards needed to be raised.

I believe that part of getting to 'Good' is about consistency. I have also always argued that two things turn a school round – behaviour and infrastructure. I had very little control of behaviour in that it had to filter down from the top, but I did have control of the department's infrastructure.

The school adopted a lesson sequence of do it now (recap/retention), new knowledge, pen to paper and reflection which was embedded throughout the school, and this was expected to be seen. Whilst the KS3 curriculum was co-constructed, I had everyone teaching the same texts. After a visit to a very well-known school, I made the department a booklet. I can't remember if I actually consulted the department about this or just made the decision. I had seen the expert way they were being used at this school and felt that, with a booklet, the provision across the department would see the pupils getting a very similar diet. I constructed most of the booklets to model the standard, as at the time 50 per cent of the department were teachers who were new to the profession. Eventually, I had members of the team co-constructing future booklets during department time. Even though I tried to make it clear on numerous occasions that the booklets were the foundation, that they could be adapted as we went through a unit, with time taken to readdress something if pupils hadn't quite grasped something, some teachers felt stripped of their autonomy and lost the sense of themselves in the classroom. They didn't work with the booklet, but simply told pupils to turn to page three and complete exercise four. The thinking behind their teaching had gone.

The plan was always for teachers to develop more and more of their own booklets over time – putting their own personality into them and having more ownership of them, accompanying them with PowerPoints if they so wished, but only when we had seen the standards rise. The year I left the school, we attained our highest ever results and I attributed this to the booklet and the way in which they had prioritised knowledge and practice. The year after I left, the results fell by about 25 to 30 per cent. Whilst I admit I was a bit of a control freak, I know that the dip in results was in part due to the loss of the structure and that same level of consistency.

Flash forward to the present day and now I work in a completely autonomous environment. The team is an incredibly experienced one. As a result, staff are mostly left to get on with their day-to-day teaching. Whilst we have a long-term plan, there are no medium- or short-term plans. Some resource sharing goes on, but people often teach different things, with a free choice of what is taught text wise, especially at KS3.

Moving from an environment of high control to complete freedom was incredibly challenging, for me, personally. As a self-confessed control freak, I like structure and organisation. I like knowing what I am doing, when I am doing it and how long I have to do it. I felt very alone to begin with, although my head of department was available any time I wanted to talk to her or ask anything of her. Now I am a year in, and having taught all year groups once through, am constructing a curriculum I see the pupils in my class moving forward with. I am in control of my curriculum.

I constantly reflect upon my situation now and feel a number of things. There has to be a happy medium. I find my freedom now too great, and perhaps when I ran my old department my control was too much. Autonomous environments can be lonely, and I think collaboration is the most powerful tool. I really miss our meetings in my old school where we would each have a copy of Alex Quigley's *Closing the Vocabulary Gap* and would discuss our thoughts about it and what they might mean for us, and the meeting where we spoke at length about religion in *A Christmas Carol*. In more autonomous environments, this doesn't happen as much, or at all.

What can I do?

If you feel trapped by scrutiny and regulations and stifled in your school, the first step would be to be honest with your line manager. Although this might be an uncomfortable situation, chances are they are feeling stifled too and will completely understand and empathise with you. There definitely needs to be a respectful dialogue about how colleagues are feeling, as sometimes head teachers can be quite removed from this and may not be aware of how their staff are feeling. If you feel unable to do this, there are other channels to feed your concerns to, such as governors or even your union representative if you feel that communication has broken down. Some schools also have staff well-being groups or a staff forum where these concerns can be voiced, but it is important that when you are discussing your feelings you are able to give specific examples and, if possible, use a solutions-focused approach to suggest how things could be improved. That way, you are not just having a 'moan', but are showing that you are serious about engaging in an open dialogue.

Of course, it is difficult for teachers to ever really have autonomy over their professional lives when school leaders themselves are not given the liberty to run their schools as they see fit because of excessive government policies. So many head teachers live in fear of accountability and being placed into a category that is deemed to be failing. So really, what agency do school leaders have and how can teachers have autonomy in their classrooms if their head feels they themselves have none?

One way to help yourself and other colleagues break out of this cycle is to seek out evidence to prove that what you are doing is not of benefit to the pupils. There is a plethora of studies and academic writings that debunk some of the practices that seem to be embedded in schools, such as the use of umpteen different coloured pens to mark work, or excessive written feedback once a week for every class you teach. Perhaps, if the leaders who are enforcing these pointless tasks are faced with the evidence, they may have a change of heart. Obviously, there is a way of doing this that is professional and subtle. Rather than standing up in a staff meeting and declaring in front of everybody that the policy is a load of rubbish, leave the article in their pigeonhole with a friendly note saying, 'I know you love your research, so I thought you might find this interesting.'

Having the confidence to exert your professional autonomy can be difficult, and sometimes being assertive and saying no can be the only way to move forward. This takes a huge amount of bravery, and if done in the wrong way can seem like you are being defiant or that you are not a team player. In this situation, it is important to know your rights. For example, at a school I worked at, I was told that I had to ring the parent of every pupil premium student in my tutor group, to remind them that it was parents' evening – despite the fact that they had already been sent letters and texts to remind them. This exercise was clearly a complete box-ticking one – something that had been devised to be wheeled out as evidence at the next inspection. I made an appointment to see my head of year and politely declined to do it, citing union guidance about admin and directed time and explaining that I thought my time might be more appropriately used on improving teaching and learning. They listened to me with good grace and agreed that it was an admin task, later emailing the rest of the year group team to tell them that they no longer needed to do it.

Of course, not all conversations of this nature will go this way, and there have been times where I have been told to 'like it or lump it'. When this happens, I tend to look for other ways in which I can be a bit more autonomous, such as choosing my own text choices at GCSE. Although this doesn't completely alleviate the frustration, I feel that it does remind me that there are other ways in which I can have agency, even if at times I have to do things I don't see the value of. Ultimately, you choose to work at a school partly because you agree with the head's ideology and ethos, so we have to trust them to do what is right – even if that sometimes jars with our own beliefs.

Autonomy is not just about having the freedom to make your own professional judgements at school. Psychologist Isha Judd writes that it is also about having 'the confidence to be ourselves, and the self-awareness to know who we are and what we want' (Judd, 2008: 18). Therefore, what is key in our own personal battle for more freedom at work is that we do not lose sight, even in the most controlling of schools, of our own moral purpose and who we are as educators. It is important that we get to know ourselves. Sometimes, when we feel trapped and unhappy, it is easy to feel like our working lives are spiralling out of control and that we are disenfranchised and ignored. Start to reflect on some of the things that you are being asked to do at work and do not agree with. Do they make a positive impact on the children? If the answer is no, then you need to speak your truth and tell your line manager about your concerns. If the answer is yes, then try to list the positive impacts and this may make you feel that it is, after all, something you can get on board with.

It is also important to sometimes challenge your beliefs and assumptions. Often, our opinions come from a habitual place, so when we are asked to do something new, it can sometimes result in the knee-jerk reaction of thinking it is wrong. Sometimes, feelings of having no autonomy are just that: feelings. You may have lots of autonomy but have not acknowledged it. It is important to find out where this thought is coming from and then to test it to see whether it is actually self-imposed. Teaching is a unique career, as teachers are growing and developing all the time. It is important to re-evaluate our perceptions of ourselves as teachers and how best we can help our pupils. Education is a landscape that is constantly shifting, and without learning and trying new things, we will not evolve as educators.

Nobody is saying that achieving freedom at school is going to be easy; it's very difficult to achieve this in a top-down institution and with a top-down government. So if it is difficult to perceive that you have autonomy at school because of restrictive school systems, one way of feeling a sense of agency might be to steer your own development out of school by engaging in reading and research in your own time and using social media networks such as Twitter to engage with other teachers in professional debates. Also, completing other training or qualifications such as a master's degree or doctorate can be extremely liberating. If things are difficult at work, it can really help to feel this sense of direction over your own development and career. I have completed three master's qualifications and am halfway through a doctorate. Studying has definitely made me feel a sense of control and improved how I feel about my career.

Many schools are now encouraging staff to personalise their own CPD and performance management targets, and this is one way that you can be more independent and individual in your own development. Ask yourself: 'What do I want to do?' and consider your own passions and interests. Although some of your targets may be predetermined or guided by school priorities, it is important that the school also meet your needs, as the relationship between school and teacher is a co-dependent one. A good school leadership will work with you to identify your needs and discover ways to meet them through training, coaching or even opportunities to lead on areas in which you have special expertise. Recently, I have heard of an increasing number of schools asking staff to complete research projects or inquiry questions, where they trial strategies with their class and discuss their findings with other departments in the school. This is a great way for teachers to have more freedom and agency and could even result in a culture shift in the school, or a change in policy if the findings are found to make a positive impact. John Tomsett and Jonny Uttley describe inquiry questions in their recent book, *Putting Staff First* (Tomsett & Uttley, 2020).

Finally, as this book goes to press, we are living through interesting times. During this COVID-19 pandemic, teachers are working from home, free from the constraints of a school environment and the normal scrutiny they have been used to. Aside from a few stories I've read about some teachers having to fill out timesheets every day for the work they are doing online, it seems teachers are being trusted to carry out their duties without interference from senior leaders. What is more, in this unprecedented situation, they are doing an excellent job. Perhaps this will herald a time of new-found respect for teachers, where their professionalism is trusted and they can just get on with their jobs. Only time will tell. But if the government wants to keep teachers in the classroom, it needs to give school leaders the dignity and freedom to do what is right for their pupils and staff.

Chapter 8
Reason to leave #8: Low salaries and high expectations

Nobody goes into teaching thinking that they are going to get rich, but many of the teachers I interviewed felt that the pay levels were not reflective of teachers' experience, qualifications, expertise and the dedication they gave to their job. In a recent survey, almost half of teachers questioned who were considering leaving the profession spoke about how the current pay framework was a factor (survey cited in *TES*, 2019b).

The average full-time teacher is officially contracted to work 38 hours a week, yet many teachers work almost double that, as it would be impossible to squeeze all of the planning, marking and paperwork they need to complete into their PPA time at school. In fact, it seems that 70 per cent of teachers are working over 50 hours a week just to keep on top of their workloads (DfE, 2019c). For many, the problems are not with the rate of pay in teaching but the sheer amount of going above and beyond and working during evenings and weekends that just seems to be a given in teaching. If a teacher's salary was divided by the hours worked rather than contracted hours, main scale teachers would be paid less than many unskilled workers – quite shocking when you consider that to qualify as a teacher you need a degree and a postgraduate qualification.

When teaching is compared to other public-service professions such as the police, the difference is stark. New police constables start their career on £20,880, which is £4000 less than newly qualified teachers. Yet within seven years, they are earning over £40,000, while teachers are stuck on £36,646. Police officers also retire on full pensions at the age of 50, whereas teachers' retirement age is in line with the general working population at 65. Many may choose to retire at 60, but they will have to accept deductions on their public service pension. In nursing, starting salaries are equal to those of teachers, yet stagnate at just £30,000 unless promotion is sought to become a teacher. Obviously, this is a travesty, as we all know how hard those in the NHS work. It perhaps demonstrates that teachers are paid reasonably well by comparison, which nobody could deny when comparing these two figures. Comparisons like these mean that the public perception of teachers may be that they are adequately paid, considering the amount of annual leave they have. Yet as well as the regular 12-hour plus days in term time, teachers often work through parts of their holidays, preparing teaching resources for the next half term or running revision sessions in school.

Of course, there is the opportunity for teachers to increase their pay by adding a TLR. However, some teachers do not want to seek promotion to a school leader position and instead would rather be rewarded for becoming experts at their craft. Previous initiatives from the government such as 'advanced skills teachers' or 'excellent teachers' rewarded expert teachers financially, while also celebrating teachers who wanted to remain in the classroom. However, these initiatives have now been abandoned and replaced by 'lead practitioner' (LP) roles, which can be financially lucrative yet are few and far between. There are also 'specialist leader in education' (SLE) roles, which provide the opportunity to work with other schools and advance your skill set but do not offer any renumeration.

Experienced teachers who are close to the top of the pay scale can feel like the forgotten. The newspapers are full of stories about golden hellos and bursaries to recruit new teachers into schools. In January 2020, the government revealed plans to raise the starting salaries of teachers in

England to £26,000, rising to £30,000 after two years' service. Although this will help with recruitment, it seems like a kick in the teeth for experienced teachers, as there were no plans from the government to make similar increases across the entire workforce (*TES*, 2020b).

A large number of the teachers I interviewed felt like the issues with renumeration were caused by performance-related pay (PRP). PRP was introduced in September 2014, which meant that pay progression based on length of service was removed and all pay progression was linked to performance. In industry, this is a common situation, where employees are rewarded in the form of bonuses. However, teachers are not call centre workers flogging kitchens or mobile phone insurance. They are working with humans whose rates of progress are entirely unpredictable.

For GCSE and year 6 primary teachers, this can be particularly unfair, as how successful they have been may be based entirely on how well their students have done in their exams. Often, the targets teachers are pushing their students towards are entirely unrealistic and do not take into account the personal experiences a student may have gone through in their schooling or the fact that they were affected for two years by staff absence. Every student has their own unique narrative, yet these are often ignored in a quest for one size fits all data analysis.

Quite understandably, this approach is making teachers frustrated and forcing them to lose the goodwill they have so often drawn from in giving up their time to run extra-curricular activities or school trips. Proponents of the system think it gives teachers the incentive to improve their teaching and increases the drive to do well. Ironically, research suggests that performance-related schemes actually have an average impact of 'just above zero months' progress' (Education Endowment Foundation, 2018). Yet other research has shown that 'permitting teachers to have a scope of quicker salary advancement will have a positive effect on pupil outcomes' (Dolton et al., 2011: 3). It will be interesting to see how schools reward teachers this year (2020) in terms of progression, now that formal examinations have been cancelled because of COVID-19 and teacher judgement is going to be used instead. Will school leaders decide to halt all teachers' pay progression or move everyone up instead?

As the government forces through the PRP guidelines, it is also ruling that schools should no longer be under any obligation to match a teacher's existing salary when they are recruiting. This could be good news for some, as teachers may be able to skip pay brackets if a head teacher is desperate to recruit, but it can also mean that if a teacher is post-threshold in their current school, it may not be a given that this will be the case if they move schools. This can make it difficult for experienced teachers to leave the schools they are in, even if they are unhappy. For some, accepting a pay cut for doing the job is not only insulting, but can be disastrous financially, particularly when there are mortgages to pay and dependents to support.

The sad fact is that many teachers are struggling to make ends meet. The National Office of Statistics (BBC, 2012) claimed that 84,000 teachers had second jobs such as tutoring. Paying for rent, utilities and childcare can be a real struggle for single parent teachers who are on the main pay scale. The Education Support Partnership is a charity that was set up to support teachers who may be suffering from financial hardship. In 2018, the number of teachers applying to the charity rose by 40 per cent (the *Independent*, 2019b).

This was not because teachers are living extravagant lifestyles, buying flashy BMWs and going on exclusive summer holidays. There are educators who are genuinely living on the breadline and struggling to feed their families. The charity warned that there are teachers 'living in sheds [and] cars and eating out of food banks'. For some teachers in the south-east, property prices are so extortionate that a teaching wage will just not cover it, particularly for those who are just excluded, by a matter of metres, from the London weighting element of pay. Kim Knappet, a former president of the National Education Union, currently volunteers at a Trussell Trust foodbank in Lewisham, and noticed that recently she has been helping more and more teachers who are in need of food and clothing for themselves and their children. She said:

> I think it's a disgrace that people with such important jobs are resorting to using food banks. We should be paying

teachers and teaching assistants a proper living wage. Teachers are receiving low staffing pay and suffering from high housing costs, which is leaving lots of them on the breadline (London News Online, 2019).

This struggle is also driving teachers into debt, with 1 in 4 having debt that worries them, 15 per cent having unsecured lending of between £5000 and £10,000, and another 19 per cent having debts of over £10,000 (Your Money Sorted, 2020).

For career changers, the struggle can be even worse. Those used to a higher wage, who have large financial commitments, can really feel the strain. It is a feeling that I remember well.

My story

Starting a PGCE and changing careers with a tiny baby is not ideal, but it was a situation I found myself in during my late 20s. My husband had just secured employment as an apprentice laboratory technician at the University of Manchester and was on a very low wage, and I had just left a well-paid job in journalism. Despite the initial pay cut, the decision had seemed like a no-brainer. I would get all the holidays off with my baby and so cut down on the childcare bills. After years of working in an industry characterised by its cut-throat attitude and lack of morals, I wanted to give something back and plough my time into a more altruistic career instead. It was unbelievably tough, though.

For the first few years, we were living hand to mouth, barely making ends meet. I remember accepting any opportunities for earning more money at school: teaching at summer schools, personal tutoring and one-to-one tuition with disadvantaged children. I even got a weekend waitressing job at one point to pay for Christmas presents and food. On one occasion, I was waiting expectantly to be paid extra in my pay packet for some hours I had done at an Easter school. We had budgeted this into our monthly income and planned to spend it on a well-earned weekend away as a family, booking in advance and only paying a deposit. When pay day came, I was horrified to see that the school's payroll hadn't put the request through on time and that it would be paid next month instead. My head of department found me in tears, and when I explained why, she very kindly gave me the money and told me to pay her back when I could. Although I felt ashamed, I was so grateful that she had helped me out.

The worst is when there is an unexpected expense, such as the washing machine breaking or a car tyre needing to be replaced. On Boxing Day one year, the house we were renting suddenly got a gas leak in one of the pipes and we had to turn the heating off in the freezing winter cold, with a very young baby. We ended up moving house hurriedly in the next few days. We couldn't afford a van to shift our belongings, so my brother and father-in-law had to help us out by doing several trips in their cars with trailers on the back!

Luckily, I am at the top of the pay scale now and my husband manages the labs at the university, so things are much more financially comfortable. However, we still don't own a house and sometimes I wonder whether we ever will! With extortionate childcare costs and rent, it's difficult to save. But I know that there are millions in much more precarious positions than me, so feel very thankful.

I feel like I am now paid enough, but I do feel a level of frustration as I stagnate at the top of the upper pay scale. For me, there seems to be no other route but senior leadership if I want to earn more money, as there are very few lead practitioner vacancies in my LEA. I also love the school I work at, so my hands are somewhat tied.

Sometimes, the general public's perception of teachers is that we like to moan a lot – especially when we get 'all of those holidays'. This won't make me popular, but I think there is an element of truth in this. I am glad I got to spend some time in industry and realise that, in fact, things aren't perfect in other jobs either. As a journalist, I worked insanely long hours, 14- to 15-hour days were the norm and I was supposed to be on call 24 hours a day. One Christmas, I turned my mobile phone off on a visit to Glasgow to spend time with my dad and turned it back on in the evening to find dozens of abusive and angry messages from the news editor, screaming at me that I needed to return to London now, as I was needed in the office. It was the year of the dreadful tsunami in Asia and it was all hands on deck. Unfortunately, the news doesn't ever sleep.

That kind of constant pressure is intense, but it set me up well to cope with the demands of teaching. There are many other stressful careers, where employees work long hours, but it can sometimes seem like they earn a lot more than teachers. I don't think I could ever go back to industry now, as the sheer joy of spending the holidays with my own children, whom I sometimes neglect a little during term time, is worth the pressure. Whenever I feel like leaving the profession, I have a look at the salaries being offered for other jobs I could apply for. This soon reminds me that we are in a fortunate position. I just wish the workload was more manageable!

For years, I didn't really think about the amount I earned until I moved to a very middle-class school in an affluent area. Many of the students had parents who were millionaires and went on extravagant foreign holidays, and their parents drove expensive Range Rovers. I remember having a chat with a year 10 boy about his aspirations and I suggested being a PE teacher to him. He scoffed and then asked me, 'Why would I want to be a teacher? When I am older, I want to drive a Porsche, not a Nissan.' This made me realise that the reason why people may not want to enter the teaching profession could be because of the impression of it being a low-status job, and this is definitely linked to salary.

Voices from the profession

Rachel Black, teacher of English
Are teachers paid enough? My contracted hours are 32.5 per week. I have usually worked my hours by some point early on Thursday, so in effect I work for free for the rest of the week.

I have been teaching for over 20 years, am at UPS3 (upper pay scale 3) and have a TLR for KS3. I wouldn't necessarily expect to work my exact hours each week, but even taking off my additional responsibility, I could not plan, teach and assess all the students I teach to even close to the required standard in my allocated hours.

I have always worked more than my paid hours. In my early years, some of my time was wasted in faffing and procrastinating, but not much, and as my career progressed and I also became a parent, my time management became highly effective. The time I'm not particularly efficient is when I'm very tired, and for me this is over 50 hours a week, or in the last week of term, when a whole new world of exhaustion appears. So I don't work more than 50 hours a week, which means I do my job well. My lessons are well planned and I mark the key things that allow me to ensure the students in my classes are learning and getting better at the things I'm teaching. I do a reasonable amount of work towards my TLR and am available to support students who need some additional support. Sometimes, I even manage to get some forward planning done. If I were paid for the hours that I need to work to do my job well, I would be paid significantly more.

In order to be a reasonable parent and maintain some relationships (with friends, family and husband), I had to work part-time for several years. I took a hit to my pay and pension because, for a while, it was only possible for me to work 35 hours a week. But I ended up being paid a part-time wage for working the full-time contracted hours.

In addition, I manage my own CPD. I reflect on ways to be better. I buy books to help me, read blogs, follow educationalists on Twitter and focus on improving my own practice. I attend free CPD that interests me. I look for ways to make my teaching better for classes that I find tricky. I apply as much of my own learning to my teaching as I can. I buy and read young adult (YA) books so that I can recommend new and interesting books to my students. Most of this is in my own time and not within my 50 hours.

I could not meet the standards teachers are held to by working my contracted hours. I am not a martyr and I manage my work and mental health well. If I'm feeling particularly stressed, I cut back. There is never a point when all my work is done, but I do what's needed to the best of my ability within the hours I set myself. Unfortunately, however, it's simply not possible to get a full-time teaching job done within my paid, contracted hours.

Anonymous, maths teacher

The reality is that I've been teaching for 16 years, and every year I seem to struggle even more. I am a single parent with a disabled daughter who lives in a residential home, which I have to pay towards. I also have another daughter at university, and although she gets help from student loans, I still need to support her to buy food and clothing. I don't want her to get a job, as she is studying medicine, the hours are too tough and the workload is too huge for her to work and stay afloat.

I work an extra job in a local pub, sometimes multiple nights a week and one day during the weekend for minimum wage, just so I can pay my mortgage and utility bills. My car is on finance and, while the monthly payments cripple me, I have to do it. Otherwise, I wouldn't be able to get to work. Sometimes, I suffer from severe back pains and I have to take painkillers to get through the teaching day, but I dare not ring and call in sick at school, as I am scared of this resulting in a meeting where I might lose my job. But there have been a couple of occasions where I had to tell my line manager I was ill because my washing machine had broken and I couldn't afford to get it fixed, so I had no clean clothes for school. I felt so ashamed and embarrassed – I have a master's degree, for goodness sake!

I do love my job, but I wish that there was a way for me to earn the amount of money for the hours I put in so that I am not constantly struggling and stressing over how I'm going to pay the next bill.

Anonymous, teacher of English

I decided to retrain as an English teacher in my 50s. I'd already had a successful teaching career in FE, spanning almost 20 years. I used to teach horticulture and I'd worked my way slowly up to being an advanced practitioner before going into teacher training.

Over time, I'd worked at a couple of universities and ended up teaching in a government-led initiative to train teachers in China for six years. As that initiative was winding down, I started to wonder what to do next. I realised I was too young to retire, and I made the decision to retrain to teach English instead.

In spite of my previous experience, I was happy to complete another PGCE, and I did an SKE (subject knowledge enhancement) course at the same time. I suppose by the time you get to your 50s, you are humble enough to realise that there are so many things you don't know. I wanted to be able to hit the ground running, especially as I knew I would only have ten years maximum in the classroom.

I was very fortunate to do my training at Northern Lights SCITT, a well-organised and well-connected organisation. Our subject lead was an amazing English teacher at Feversham Academy, whose English results had been excellent for a long time. The training year was as tough as it gets, even for an old hand like me, but I found that the English bursary and the loan were enough to live on.

I was still very worried about getting a job, because you really don't see that many people over the age of 50 starting out in a teaching role in schools. However, I was delighted to be offered the first job I applied for and it has been a very fulfilling experience.

The financial side was very tough in the first year and I was lucky that with my previous experience the school didn't put me on the bottom rung of the pay scale. Also, I had no mortgage to pay, which was very lucky, because life still got in the way as it often does. My son was very ill for a number of months and was diagnosed with a rare and potentially life threatening illness. We had to support him through this, and it was really tough going.

It reminded me of the first time I'd come into teaching, when there were many times I didn't have the money to put any petrol in the car. Things have got much better now I'm an RQT (Recently Qualified Teacher), because the pay feels much better already. However, it did make me reflect on how hard it is financially to come into teaching. On our WhatsApp group, my fellow trainees would talk about how tough they were finding it, and money was one of the factors that made people feel like dropping out. I felt really sorry for one of my friends who was saving up to get married and had to work in a pizza delivery shop at night to fund his wedding.

People cite workload as the main reason for early-career teacher dropout, but I honestly think financial reasons are just as much to blame.

Niamh Doherty, head of inclusion and SENCo

A few Mondays ago, I got a call asking me to attend a court hearing. That day I also comforted the parent of a former pupil after the pupil self-harmed at their new secondary school. I interviewed for a teaching assistant position, modelled how to run an intervention, met with a family and other professionals to discuss the legalities of a child's provision, and taught in year 1. My friend, an actuary accountant, assessed the risk of some financial investments. The average actuary accountant earns £70,000.

That Tuesday, I spent most of the morning with a distraught pupil, her mother and the police. In the afternoon, I attended a leadership meeting. My head teacher and school business manager told us about their meeting with the LEA to discuss our deficit budget. We don't have midday supervisors anymore. We've gone from one teaching assistant in every class to one (often part-time) shared between three to four classes, and now we're going to end our contracts with our specialist music, PE and MFL (modern foreign languages) teachers. We'll still be in deficit. My friend, a tax director, wrote a detailed tax plan. The average tax director earns £85,742.

On Wednesday, I taught in year 6, and whilst I was teaching a child made a disclosure. I rang the Multi Agency Safeguarding Hub. I had a cry. I taught the nuances of the modal verb. I was called from class to de-escalate a situation where a distressed child had arrived at school and promptly tried to scale the fence to leave again. The child's mum was crying and the child was crying. I'd already cried that morning and really do try to keep crying for when I get home. When I got back to class, I taught the nth term. My friend, a PR manager, organised a party in a chicken shop attended by some celebrities until 1 p.m. Then they brought round the drinks trolley. The average PR manager earns £43,574 plus bonuses.

Thursday is my favourite day because I teach an English booster after school and a nurture group in the afternoon. After the English booster, I went back into the office I had spent the rest of the day in and, together with the rest of the leadership team, decided how we would keep our school open when schools closed. We had waited all day for the list of key workers and estimated up to 70 per cent of our families could be eligible, depending on the criteria. Shouldn't be too much of a problem, as our pupil numbers had plummeted from nearly 700 to around 200 that week. My friend, a director of product management, prepared a report to keep the stakeholders up to date on product process and progress. The average director of product management earns £92,692.

We closed our gates on Friday afternoon. I tried to comfort children, I tried to comfort parents, I tried to comfort my staff. I didn't have any answers or really know what was coming. Since then, I've done the same as every other school leader. We've switched to online learning (had a scary security breach), lost members of our school community (should we send flowers?), phoned our families, written policies, made food parcels and so much more. My friend, a vice president of sales, designed a new and (hopefully) more effective sales strategy for a beauty brand. The average vice president of sales earns £109,278.

The average member of a primary school leadership team earns £41,570.

What can I do?

Aside from waiting to move up through the pay scale or seeking promotion or TLRs, there seems little that teachers can do about poor pay. Thankfully, the DfE has made recommendations that teacher pay should rise by 3 per cent for September 2020, which would make this the 'biggest sustained uplift in teacher pay since 2005' (*Schools Week*, 2020). If this goes ahead, UPS3 would go from £40,490 to £42,502.

Figure 21: Proposed DfE pay rises for September 2020 (Source: Schools Week, 2020)

	New Structure	Existing Structure	Change (£)	Change (%)
M1	£26,000	£24,373	£1,627	6.7%
M2	£27,820	£26,298	£1,522	5.8%
M3	£29,767	£28,412	£1,355	4.8%
M4	£31,851	£30,599	£1,252	4.1%
M5	£34,081	£33,009	£1,071	3.2%
M6	£36,870	£35,971	£899	2.5%
U1	£38,595	£37,654	£941	2.5%
U2	£40,025	£39,049	£976	2.5%
U3	£41,502	£40,490	£1,012	2.5%

With the government's promise to raise starting salaries to £30k by 2022/23, it is proposed that UPS3 will rise to £43,953. The DfE claims that these pay rises will help to retain more than 1000 teachers each year and that to help this, they may simplify and streamline the pay structure and banish the UPS altogether, to create just a single classroom teacher pay range. How this might link to PRP is unknown, as teachers have historically had to fight hard to move through the UPS, filling in copious amounts of paperwork to prove that they are worthy of progression. The average UK graduate starting salary is £30,000 (High Fliers Report, 2020), so the pay rise proposed by the DfE would bring teaching in line with this. Furthermore, at the top of the pay scale, £41,502 puts teachers around £10,000 to £11,000 over the average monthly UK salary. It is great that the DfE is recognising that teachers deserve to be paid adequately for the vital job they do. However, there are also other things that teachers can do to help themselves financially.

For some teachers, one big expense can be their car, as often teachers need it to commute to school. Many car dealers, such as Motor Source Group, offer discounts to teachers and lecturers of up to 30 per cent on a new car, and some insurance suppliers also offer reduced rates for teachers. Another way of saving money on transportation costs is to car share with colleagues who may live close by. In addition, if you work for an LEA, you may be offered discounted use of council facilities such as gyms and leisure centres. You can even get a 10 to 30 per cent discount on mobile phone contracts through schemes for public service workers. There are also several websites where teachers can look for bargains and special deals such as discountsforteachers.co.uk or perksforteachers. co.uk. Always worth a look!

If, like many teachers, you find it difficult to afford to go on holiday during peak season, it may be worth applying for the International Teacher Identity Card. The card is an internationally recognised ID card that can get you access to some fantastic discounts around the world, such as up to 40 per cent off flights and 5 per cent off travel insurance with STA Travel. There are also thousands of benefits worldwide on accommodation, transport and food. Hilton also offers great discounts for teachers on some of their hotels too.

One thing that some teachers can forget about is that we do not have to pay tax on professional subscriptions or union fees. As this is not automatic and you have to let HMRC know, this money often goes unclaimed. Although some companies will offer to do this on your behalf for a fee, it is free for you to do yourself and also quite straightforward. According to Money Saving Expert (2018), the average teacher's tax rebate is between £200 and £250, so it is well worth doing.

There are also things that teachers can do to boost their income which may take some time but will help develop you as a practitioner. One of these options is to apply to become an exam marker. This can not only be lucrative, but can develop your subject knowledge and understanding of how pupils can achieve the top grades at GCSE. I interviewed teachers up and down the country who told me about how the money they earn from their exam marking pays for their family holiday the year after, or for Christmas presents. Another option is to do some private tutoring. To do this, you will have to register yourself as self-employed for a second job with HMRC, so that you can pay the correct amount of tax, but with tutees paying a minimum of £25 per hour, it is well worth it. Another option might be to write articles for education publications or online websites that pay for teacher contributions. While this is unlikely to make you into a millionaire, it can supplement your income somewhat and be an interesting experience to boot.

With things moving in the right direction with teachers' pay and the DfE's attempts to lower expectations of workload, I hope that we may be entering a better time for teachers. I am certain that with the excellent work teachers are doing caring for the children of key workers during the COVID-19 crisis, their status in the eyes of the public will rise and there will be support for the profession the likes of which has not been seen for decades. We have always known how wonderful and dedicated teachers are, but parents are now also realising this as they struggle to educate their own children at home. Hopefully, the sacrifice and contribution of teachers will never be forgotten, and our pay will reflect this.

Chapter 9
Reason to leave #9: Promotion pressure

The context

For an experienced teacher who has worked hard to reach the UPS, it can be quite frustrating to know that there is no further to go unless you wish to take on the role of head of department or senior leader. This frustration was clearly felt by the participants on the teacher retention survey (DfE, 2018), where teachers said that they felt trapped by the fact that there was 'no opportunity for further salary increases because of the public sector pay cap' (DfE, 2018: 27). As discussed in the previous chapter, teachers do not come into the profession with the intention of becoming millionaires. However, knowing that the salary you are earning after ten years in the classroom will not change for the rest of your career can be quite depressing.

Of course, teachers can take on TLRs in schools, which can boost their earnings, but often these are linked to curriculum management and progression within subject areas, or with more traditional SLT roles. For some teachers, this is not the direction they want to take in their careers; jumping onto the treadmill of promotion is not for them. Inevitably, as educators move further up the management ladder, their time in the classroom diminishes and more of their school day is taken up with administrative tasks and paperwork. A position in senior leadership can be extremely rewarding, as you get to directly shape and influence the direction of the school and really make a difference on a more strategic level, to both pupils and staff. However, for those whose main appeal of the profession is the interaction they get from working in the classroom every day with the students, the traditional route to leadership might not be for them. Much of the frustration the teachers felt in the research was the lack of routes for progression for those who would like to still retain a focus on teaching.

In 1998, the Labour government realised that this frustration was a significant factor in the retention of experienced teachers and introduced the role of 'advanced skills teacher' (AST) for experienced practitioners who could demonstrate excellent classroom practice. This post straddled the fence between classroom teacher and SLT and required those in the role to support teaching colleagues within their own and other schools in the local area. Tony Blair called it 'a new grade of teachers to recognise the best' (Manifesto of the Labour Party, 1997). ASTs were paid on an 18-point pay spine – identical to the first points in the leadership pay scale – giving expert teachers parity with assistant and deputy heads.

Although applying for the role could be quite daunting, teachers welcomed its creation as a way for them to remain in the classroom while gaining promotion. This kind of role is also a fantastic way to improve the teaching and learning in the school as a whole. As the McKinsey Report (2007) found, the only way to improve outcomes is to ensure that all children receive a high-quality education, and this education can only be as good as the teachers. So a role like this, where expert teachers can share their skills and improve the pedagogy of others, would help to improve teaching and help students get better outcomes. Yet in 2013, the Conservative government abolished this role without a succession plan, leaving the 5000 teachers who held the position around the country without their role.

In 2015, the DfE announced that a new role would be created, which was similar to the AST role but called a 'lead practitioner' (LP), where, outside of London, teachers could earn up to £62,735 while still spending most of their time teaching. The rest of their work would focus on CPD, mentoring, and teaching and learning – both in their own schools and in other schools in the LEA. However, an LP's pay packet is pricey. With school budgets under immense pressure, few schools may be able to afford to shell out such a substantial sum for a teacher, and instead would pay an assistant head this money, adding the duties that an LP would do to the assistant head's duties. These roles are few and far between. In a search at the height of recruitment season across the whole of the North West of England, there were only four LP roles advertised. Clearly, there needs to be more of these roles available or different avenues of promotion created for experienced teachers that don't require the teachers to move out of the classroom.

For those of us who are perfectly happy with our salary and content to stay in the classroom, the pressure from others to seek promotion can be a factor in making us dissatisfied with our career choices. An NQT recently asked me how long I had been teaching, and when I replied 13 years, she looked at me incredulously and said, 'And you're still a classroom teacher?' I felt myself blushing and feeling compelled to tell her my work history – that I had been in a leadership position and had made the decision to step down myself, as, at the time, it wasn't for me. I felt embarrassed and ashamed that in the eyes of this ambitious young teacher, I hadn't made a success of my career. As a profession, we seem to celebrate teaching success based on how quickly a teacher can sprint into an SLT position, and when you are looking around at your contemporaries who trained with you and noticing that they are almost all head teachers or deputy head teachers, it can be difficult not to feel that you have failed somewhat.

Unfortunately, the teaching profession does not always seem to reward career teachers who just want to do a great job and share their good practice with others. Therefore, people like me feel the pressure to apply for a management role, as they feel like this is what they should be doing, and that this is the only way to progress and develop their pedagogy in some way. But when they get there and face the reality of the job, they can feel torn by the dichotomy between being a good leader and a good teacher. Resource planning and lesson preparation can often take a back seat to policy writing and whole school strategic planning. When you are somebody who prides yourself on ploughing all your energies into teaching, this can be a really difficult pill to swallow. In my interviews with teachers, I spoke to so many who had stepped down from leadership because they felt their teaching was suffering. They had made the conscious decision to go back to classroom teaching and become an expert practitioner. Perhaps if more roles for experienced teachers – with no management responsibilities – were developed, teachers would not feel pushed into applying for roles that their heart isn't really in. I felt this pressure too and it absolutely wasn't the right time for me.

My story

I was that super ambitious NQT who wanted to be a head as quickly as possible – without even really knowing what a head teacher actually does. This came, I think, from a perception in my own mind that after leaving a very glamorous, impressive sounding job, I was slumming it a little bit by starting right at the bottom of a new career. For me, the interaction with the students was the thing I really enjoyed about the job; I prided myself in creating lessons that I thought they would enjoy doing and from which they would learn a lot. When I became head of English, I started to notice that my planning was becoming non-existent and I was relying on ready-made lessons from other teachers, sometimes not even looking at them properly until I was actually teaching them. Instead of interacting with the class, I was increasingly setting them independent tasks and sitting static, chained to my desk, completing admin tasks and data analysis or answering emails. I had gone from being a great teacher to being an absent one. I may have been in the classroom, but I wasn't really THERE, and I hated every minute.

When I made the decision to step down, move schools and return to the classroom, I went to see the head and told her I had an interview. She laughed at me and said, 'So you are stepping down to go back to the classroom…why?' Her disdain was clear. She simply couldn't understand why somebody would want to make this move. But it was totally the right decision for me.

Over the last six years, my focus has been solely on honing my skills in the classroom, and I feel like my practice has developed in leaps and bounds. I have embraced research, completed a master's in psychology, and become a doctoral candidate in education. While doing this, I've enjoyed writing for *TES*, publishing journal articles and speaking at conferences – none of which I feel I would have had time for had I stayed in my management position. Of course, many in leadership positions manage all of this and I applaud them. But with young children also, I really struggled. Stepping down from my leadership role also allowed me to specialise and use my expertise in teaching more able pupils to secure a whole school role coordinating challenge across the curriculum, and to free time up to become a staff governor.

Interestingly, moving to a new school made me realise that somebody's career path doesn't necessarily have to be a straight road; it can be a long and winding path. When I met my department, I discovered that no fewer than five of us had been in school leadership positions, many having served as assistant head teachers. For their own varying reasons, they had decided to step down also, but as they assured me, just because I wasn't ready then doesn't mean I will never be.

Today, once again, I am beginning to feel the itch. I want something more, and although an LP role would be absolutely perfect, they seem to be rarely advertised in my local area. Once again, SLT seems like an attractive position, but also one of the only viable ones.

Voices from the profession

James Hodge, deputy head teacher (former lead practitioner)

I became an LP six years into my teaching practice. I had trained on the School Direct programme at an affluent rural community school, where I was swiftly promoted to head of media studies in my NQT year. It was a brilliant environment to learn to teach in: a focus on life and world learning that fed into exam teaching and produced outstanding results; a leadership team that was supportive and empowered staff, allowing them autonomy; and a community of high-performing and research-engaged teachers who were always seeking to develop their practice.

However, after six years, I was ready to move into a new role higher up in management. I knew that I wanted to pursue the academic pathway as opposed to the pastoral, and was recommended a plethora of options: the two that I gave most consideration to were head of English and senior leadership. For me, however, neither was the ideal fit. Having been a HoD on a smaller scale, for me head of English was too admin heavy and focused on data and didn't interest me, as I am an enthusiastic classroom practitioner. The SLT, on the other hand, was too far removed from the classroom – less teaching time and more removed from the community of teachers I loved.

It was then that I discovered the role of LP: essentially, a new take on the AST roles made popular in the 2000s. The LP role sounded like an ideal one. We would essentially be subject experts, focusing on supporting HoDs in developing curriculum and supporting teaching (both coaching current members of staff and training NQT, TeachFirst and PGCE trainees). Our primary role would be research-based, trying out and developing best practice to roll out across the department and develop the curriculum in line with new Ofsted and research requirements. There was a whole school element to the role too: a literacy focus alongside regular contribution to teaching and learning briefings and CPD. Ultimately, the school would employ us across the wider academy chain to develop curriculum and teaching across schools. This ticked many of the desired elements I wanted in my new position: a role where my creativity and knowledge could be used to support teaching on a wider level beyond my own classroom in a new working environment where I could establish myself as more of a 'middle leader'. The school context was very different: an inner-city London school that had achieved bad results the previous year.

In many ways, the job was a rewarding one. The department was open to many of my approaches – especially with my having been an exam marker the previous summer. There was an urgent need for planning, which I had in spadefuls, and a more contemporary approach to teaching.

There was little cohesion between classrooms – what was taught and how it was taught – caused by an unclear learning journey. I enjoyed helping to develop more of an educational philosophy for the team and creating a curriculum that was more in line with current ideas. Furthermore, the whole school literacy project was interesting, and I enjoyed the research-based nature of it. However, the real privilege for me was working with so many trainees who were keen to learn and develop. Seeing them go from 'baby teachers' to 'fully flown practitioners ready to fly the nest' was hugely rewarding.

However, the role that had been presented to applicants as a research-focused and autonomous one was soon revealed to be a different beast altogether. That isn't to say it bore no resemblance, but that the focus was entirely different to that promised. Firstly, as is typical in many schools, the workload was huge, with a timetable that was barely reduced. This led to 7 a.m. starts and 7 p.m. finishes, which I wouldn't have minded had other issues not started to arise. For one, there was the ongoing 'organic' nature of the role. I was introduced on day one as a 'teacher trainer', a role entirely different to that on my job specification. There was no clear vision as to what the role would be day to day. Different bits and bobs would arise, but it fast became apparent that what the school had really wanted was an experienced teacher who would take the leadership pay to stay in the long run.

Staff turnover was high, and it was clear why: the huge workload combined with excessive and intensive staff scrutiny and an absolute focus on exam results and little else. This created many obstacles to my additional role outside of the classroom: the sheer amount of marking; the constant prepping for observations; the endless 'extra' admin that needed completing. These factors meant there was little time to really stop, research and think. Furthermore, my position within the school meant that I had very little authority or influence: the head of English had never been informed about what an LP's role would be, had such a backward educational philosophy and was so resistant to change that my efforts were often wasted. The SLT was inexperienced and only sought quick and immediate fixes instead of carefully tried and tested research-style interventions. There was little trust, little support and an absolute resistance to anything new. I left after two terms after being headhunted in April by a prestigious ITT department with whom I had worked during my mentoring.

If I were offered the role of LP again elsewhere, I would certainly consider it, but it is a role that needs to be employed carefully, with a clear vision and support. A management model where an LP has a clear job to do that supports the HoD and is supported by the SLT, which is open and will back up new ideas, would be an excellent one, especially when given the time needed. Speaking to other LP friends, this is much more the case in other schools, where LPs are essentially associate SLT.

If you want to become an LP, the first tasks sit with you. Take pride in your teaching and pedagogy day to day in your classroom. Be creative, try new things, go off-curriculum and strike the balance between outstanding life learning and excellent exam results. Ensure you constantly read and develop your practice, and use the brilliant teachers in your school, on Twitter, or at CPD events, to learn and grow. Try to contribute academically on a whole school level and really embed yourself into a school culture. You need to be outstanding in every sense of the word. Secondly, really scrutinise your school choice. Find somewhere that fits with your educational philosophy, avoid 'exam factories' and ensure that the school wants to support and develop you, utilising you meaningfully and effectively. The LP is such an important role: if you want to lead teachers forward and improve school-wide practice, this could be the role for you!

Fi Brewer, teacher of English

In 2018, I moved schools. Deeply unhappy in the school I'd taught in for the last six years and full of self-doubt, I walked away, leaving my responsibilities behind. I was almost instantly much happier, but I was also aware that it was, well, not as stimulating. I knew that if I'd stayed at my last school, I would have been driven out of teaching. Yet I also knew deep down that I was soon going to feel under-utilised, frustrated and stifled in my new school, and worried that, again, I'd want to leave.

But I was determined to stay in the career I love. To keep myself stimulated, here are some of the things I did:

1. Say 'I'll do that!'

There are always bits and bobs that need doing in schools, and if you keep an ear open or ask the right people, there are bound to be tasks floating around that you could do. I took on some curriculum planning for our SLD (severe learning difficulties) unit, which was interesting and manageable, but challenging. It also led me to work with different people in school, giving me a wider network of close colleagues.

2. Ask 'Could I have a bash at…?'

Similar to no. 1, but more forward, I've offered to do things for my HoD and SLT: construct new SOW designs, deliver department training, analyse mock exam data. Unsurprisingly, I've yet to be told no to anything, because, let's be honest, I'm saving them a job, or at least reducing it. I've focused on some of my areas of strength, but also brushed up on my weak areas. Importantly, I'm not obliged to, so can step back if I need to.

3. Venture into the outside world

Following WomenEd's 10% Braver, I started to put myself forward for things outside of school. I started subtly contacting *TES* and my subject association to pitch articles. I wouldn't have to promote them myself, and unless I mentioned it to colleagues or people happened to spot my name, no one would know. It was a nice way of challenging myself without being as exposed as I would be if I did something in school. Bolstered a bit by a couple of published pieces, I offered to do a five-minute presentation at a local TeachMeet, and once I'd proved I could do that, this grew into submissions for national conferences – a whole new level of challenge!

4. Wider reading and learning

This is the real game changer for me. Again, I started small – Teacher Tapp and Twitter – but this rapidly grew into conferences, online courses and books. I found that the more I understood what was happening in my students' brains, the more interesting teaching became. The job that wasn't very stimulating was suddenly really, really interesting, because I had a framework through which I could analyse and understand the impact of my teaching decisions and refine them in order to become a better teacher.

These and more saved me and helped me fall back in love with teaching again; there's not a chance I want to do anything else.

Anonymous, teacher of English

My first school was a large state comprehensive in Essex, where I worked as a classroom teacher for two years. I was keen to 'progress' quickly and started to look for new roles in only my second year; I was convinced that moving schools for a new role would be better for my CV. So, in 2003, I moved to become an assistant head of year, with the intention of following a pastoral pathway to head of year and then SLT with pastoral link. But with the introduction of the new TLR system, with its focus on pupil progress becoming the responsibility of the school, all assistant heads of year were made redundant and moved back to departmental roles. Support staff were given assistant head of year roles instead, with one head of year per key stage. I personally feel this was a massive change in the ethos of education that has had long-term negative effects on the well-being of students.

Instead, I moved into a departmental role as key stage coordinator for English at KS5. The role was much more challenging in terms of my subject knowledge, but less challenging emotionally. Department roles are always a source of conflict, I think. Although we work as a team, it is hard to be the one in charge, especially in an English faculty, where teams are large. Certainly, I felt that as a teacher early in my career, there was some resentment of my role, as I lacked experience. I still feel there is a sense that experience trumps everything in teaching – until you reach a 'certain age' and then people are a bit more dismissive again. After introducing a new A level successfully, three years later I moved into second in department, initially covering a maternity leave and then later taking on the role permanently. My HoD told me of his intention to retire and it was suggested I would be a natural successor, but I found out the next day that I was pregnant. I just didn't feel I could balance both roles, so a new HoD was appointed and I was invited to join the interview process whilst on maternity leave. I acted up as HoD during my pregnancy when the HoD became unwell, and then remained as second in charge on a part-time contract when I returned. The new HoD was supportive of part-time staff having TLR responsibilities, but this has not been the norm in my teaching experience.

However, I felt a bit lost under the new regime and found it hard to balance being someone who had been in charge with being classed as 'part-time'. The new HoD and I had differences, and the team felt really unhappy. We ended up having an Ofsted inspection where we had anticipated 'Good' to 'Outstanding' but were given 'Requires Improvement'. The pressure was insane. Seven out of the thirteen staff left, and I was considering my next move. Financially, I needed the salary with the TLR I held, but was really unhappy and had lost my confidence as a middle leader. After finding out that I was pregnant again, I decided to take a step back to three days a week and go back to being a classroom teacher.

Later, alongside this, I was offered a new role as whole school literacy coordinator, and I negotiated being directly managed by the head and sitting in with the SLT. I then took over running the school library after the librarian team left. I absolutely loved it, but it was hard work and took everything I had. I was completely exhausted, decided that teaching must be the issue, and left, with my plan being to be a cake baker.

I ran a business making afternoon tea and party cakes for six months, and was then asked to help a former colleague teaching at a sixth form college. This was the best job I ever had. But the sixth form sector is impossible to work in, the pay is rubbish and the hours awful.

A friend rang to speak to me about a two-day-a-week job at a large comprehensive in Essex – my catchment school. It was an 'Outstanding' school with an established leadership, so I went for it. I've been there now for four years. There's politics and department dramas, but they aren't mine. I spend most of my time in my room teaching and I don't engage with the bigger picture. I've been paired with another teacher (an NQT) and we are happily replanning a SOW for year 7, with a focus on engaging and enthusing the kids. It's a revelation. My department sees me as the old, part-time lady and I'm not really part of the office gossip of who said or did what, which is funny, as I am so used to being in the centre of it all and I could probably add quite a bit. I like my back seat, however. Every now and again, I bite and they look at me, shocked that I might have seen it all before, but I then leave at 3.30 and don't work at home, so I've got a good balance.

I've also worked in teacher training for 13 years and deliver subject sessions every Thursday. Increasingly, I see my trainees leave the profession after four years; they want a better balance. Increasingly, I'm also often asked to train English teachers who haven't got an English degree. Maybe there's a link? What I do know is that I work with trainees in my school and they are all amazing, but they find the work–life balance of being mum and teacher nigh on impossible. One even worked out that she'd earn more doing a night-time supermarket job once she factored in childcare.

So what can I tell you? Teaching is ace – being a manager and responding to the whims of a leader or Ofsted not so much. You are encouraged to move up and along the pay scale and take on responsibility, but you do a lot for free first, and age can be against you. Experience is key, but not too much, as older women aren't always recognised, especially if they are part-time. Lots of teachers fall into roles because they need the money and then they are trapped. You can't leave the role, but are you still as effective after a long time of doing the same thing? I suggest we are not good at reflection on this at all. People can be very defensive of their roles.

Being in my classroom with the kids is all that matters and the only bit I like!

Anonymous, teacher of English

My teaching career has been subject to rather a lot of moving around because of my partner's job. I have taught for 12 years and have had a range of different roles, which have been helpful in enabling me to understand what I enjoy and do best within education. I've been a head of year, which I didn't really enjoy, a key stage coordinator, which I did, and an LP, which I liked the best.

My LP role was at an academy and I was responsible for leading CPD, both in-house and in other settings; mentoring and training large cohorts of School Direct trainees; supporting staff who fared poorly in observations and work scrutiny; and developing the direction of teaching and learning within the English department. The role also placed me on the leadership scale and made me feel that my career was moving in the right direction, allowing me to fully develop and use the expertise I had developed.

However, relocating to Wales, where funding in schools is seemingly even more dire than in England, has meant a return to being 'just' a teacher. I don't wish to sound dismissive here and I intend no disrespect to teachers generally, but I have always been ambitious, and the experience I've accrued feels, to be completely frank, wasted. I'm bored. But where to go now in a system without the spare funding for roles like LP?

My opportunities for progression are now limited to leading a year group or a department. I know pastoral is not for me. As an English teacher, the idea of being a HoD is also daunting. All the English HoDs I know, many of them my contemporaries who qualified at the same time as me, seem miserable. There is the enormous pressure for results, often a large cohort of staff to manage, and a colossal amount of paperwork. Then there is the challenge of actually securing a HoD role in the first place.

In my current school, there are two key stage coordinators who seem to be lined up to take over from our soon-to-retire department head. If I were to apply externally, there are usually internal candidates with proven track records, and many schools understandably take the 'better the devil you know' approach rather than taking a risk on an unknown newbie.

Being back to teaching rather than leading has become intensely frustrating. I sit on my hands in meetings, not wishing to appear arrogant or a know-it-all. But I watch as bad decisions are made and poor leadership impacts negatively on pupil progress and my own workload. It's difficult to make suggestions without seeming critical, and my job has become repetitive and dull. I accepted an additional responsibility leading pedagogy whole school for an almost insultingly low 'bursary' payment just to give myself something to do that interests me.

I've taken the decision to apply externally for HoD roles, despite the fact I'm not even sure I want them, just to escape the frustration I am currently feeling.

What can I do?

The fantastic thing about education is that it is always moving so quickly. New opportunities are always developing – if you are willing to embrace them. The traditional leadership and management opportunities in schools are beginning to transform, and as schools are put under more scrutiny, the remit of SLT members becomes too big for them to manage, meaning there are smaller roles available for teachers who are willing to have a go at something different. These roles might not come with a huge TLR point, but they will also not have the same level of accountability or hike in workload that traditional management roles as a middle or senior leader will have. A job like this might involve taking responsibility across the school for the coordination and organisation of extra-curricular activities, or tracking and improving outcomes for a particular group of students such as pupil premium or the most able pupils.

Education policy is currently fairly fast moving, and in September 2020, one of the biggest restructurings of how NQTs are supported will be implemented across England. The Early Career Framework will see NQTs being given two years of school and government support rather than the traditional year, and will also re-emphasise the importance of mentors, providing them with training and support. This policy will create a lot of different positions in schools, including mentors and mentor training and support roles, as schools will be evaluated on the support they are providing to their new teachers during inspections.

If these kinds of roles are not available and it is the need to be challenged and developed that is driving your decision to want to leave rather than financial renumeration, there are many opportunities in schools for you to get involved with or lead. Volunteering to assist at music and drama performances is really good fun. Helping to coach a sports team allows you to see another side to the students you teach, which you might not necessarily see in your classroom.

If you have a passion for teaching and learning and research, why not volunteer to run a research or journal club at your school, where you meet with teachers from other departments and discuss a piece of research, go away and trial some of the strategies you discussed with your classes, returning at the end of the half term to assess the impact? Delivering department or whole school CPD can also be a very rewarding experience. Though nerve-wracking the first time you do it, it's a chance for you to share something you are really passionate about and to demonstrate your expertise.

Organising school trips or even going on a residential trip or exchange is also great for personal development and adds another dimension to your practice. I have been lucky enough to go on several exchange trips to Germany and France with the MFL teams and I learned so much from the experience.

Although in an ideal world these roles and activities would have a monetary reward attached to them, schools just cannot afford to pay their staff for every single thing that they do. Budgets are tight, but if you get involved in things in school, when a role with a TLR does come up, you will definitely be considered more seriously for the job if you have already been involved in whole school activities and initiatives. Anyway, as stated at the start of this chapter, while there are a few teachers out there who came into education for the money, there are many who are sitting at the top of the pay scale and crying out for some development opportunities. Many of the experienced teachers I spoke to told me that they felt 'forgotten', and that opportunities only seemed to be offered to younger, newer teachers, as they were perceived to be more 'keen'. Good leaders will provide opportunities for all of their staff, but if you find yourself feeling frustrated and needing a new challenge, speak to your line manager or SLT link member. There are always opportunities in schools for teachers; it's just that they might not know that you want them!

Chapter 10
Reason to leave #10: The grass is greener myth

Deciding to leave teaching is a huge commitment; it may feel like a huge waste of training, expertise and money, as training to become a teacher is not cheap. In the DfE teacher retention research referred to several times throughout this book (DfE, 2018), teachers who had left the profession spoke about their upset and guilt at the impact their departure might have on their pupils, particularly those in their forms and exam classes. They felt a sense of disappointment in themselves for not having been able to carry on, and the knowledge that there is a shortage of teachers entering the profession just exacerbated this. Some wanted a new challenge that schools just could not provide, but for others, problems outlined in this book forced their hand.

There is no doubt that teaching can be a stressful career, with long working hours, though the holidays somewhat make up for the long term-time hours. Undoubtedly, there is occasionally the need to complete marking and planning during the holidays and weekends, but after a few years of developing your time management skills in school, this should diminish. When you have children of your own, the ease of not needing to find childcare during the school holidays is fantastic, as I see many friends in industry struggling to juggle this between family members. Also, although some may argue that teaching is still not in line with other graduate starting salaries, it is still one of the most financially secure jobs available. Now more than ever, job security is something to be extremely thankful for. During the COVID-19 pandemic, thousands of people have been furloughed from work on around 80 per cent of their wages, and many self-employed people have been unable to claim any help at all from the government, leaving them facing financial ruin. Teachers have been lucky to still be paid in full and given the opportunity to work from home.

Teachers have many transferrable skills that could be applied to a range of different jobs. Of those who were questioned in the research (DfE, 2018), over half of the ex-secondary teachers and a third of the primary teachers had stayed in roles that were related to teaching, such as tutoring, consultancy or teacher training. Some took up roles related to the subject they taught, such as computer coding or accounting, and others went for a complete change and were working in a diverse range of careers, from photography to engineering. Yet over a quarter of the participants questioned were not working at the time of the interview, as they had failed to find a position that paid as much money or suited their skill set.

Some teachers have only ever really worked in a school. In fact, since they were about four years of age, school and education institutions are all they have ever really known. Therefore, it can be difficult to know what life is really like in other careers. This may be an unpopular opinion, but I can corroborate it with personal experience and testaments from other teachers who have worked outside of education: there are many other jobs that are as difficult as teaching, where you are required to work as many hours in stressful circumstances and sometimes for lower pay. Sometimes leaving teaching is not the magical antidote it appears to be, and there is so much about the profession that people miss when they leave. This is why thousands of teachers return to the profession every year (DfE, 2020). Sometimes the grass just isn't greener, as much as we may like to think it is.

In the DfE research (2018), many former teachers lamented the loss of the interaction they had with students in the classroom and making a difference to young people's lives, though most did state that they felt less stress and that there was more flexibility and less pressure in their new careers. There are undoubtedly many people who have left the teaching profession and would never go back, but when I interviewed people with this view, they conceded that they wished they had been provided with the support and guidance to stay in the classroom in the first place.

Like many teachers, I trained to become a teacher later on, after a successful career in industry. Teachers who do this are often under no illusion about how challenging teaching can be, but they have been in similar situations in a previous career, so they are able to see that long hours, poor work–life balance and accountability are not just problems unique to teaching. My career in journalism certainly set me up for many of the taxing situations I have experienced in the classroom.

My story

When I was 14 and choosing my options at secondary school, I remember sitting through the obligatory appointment with a careers advisor who told me that my aspirations for becoming a national newspaper journalist were ridiculous and that people from where I came from just didn't do jobs like that. Of course, this made me even more bloody-minded, so when I was in my last year in university, I applied for a prestigious scholarship with a national tabloid newspaper in London. They would give me a job as a graduate trainee journalist and also pay for me to undertake the Postgraduate Diploma in Newspaper Journalism at City University – the training ground for journalists in the national sector. Clearly, I jumped at the chance and was delighted to prove all the doubters wrong. But the dream job soon became a nightmare.

Firstly, the salary was extremely low. I earned £15,000 a year and had to pay for rent, transport, utilities and food in central London with this tiny sum. The newspaper had little sympathy – it was almost like it was a test they were subjecting me to. On several occasions, I was expected to spend my own money on things and claim them through expenses, which could often take weeks to appear. On one such occasion, it was announced that a member of the rock band Status Quo had been diagnosed with cancer and I was tasked with attending his apartment with the biggest bunch of flowers I could buy and presenting them to him on behalf of the paper. At the time, I had about £15 left in my bank account and I knew that this just wouldn't cut it, so I had to explain my predicament to the deputy news editor, who screamed at me and threw a £50 note at me to use instead. There were times when I was asked to get taxis to places on the other side of London just to deliver things to more senior journalists who were on a 'job'. All out of my own pocket of course. I have never been so destitute as a teacher or struggled for cash like I did during that time. Although some might balk at the £25,000 starting salary in teaching, this seemed like riches to me!

The working hours in journalism were also horrific. As detailed in a previous chapter, you weren't even off duty on Christmas day, and if you failed to answer the phone when called by the news desk, you were in serious trouble. An average working day for me would be to arrive at the office at around 9 a.m., working until lunch, where I would usually meet an informant, contact or Z-list celebrity and spend an hour eating and gleaning story ideas from them. I would then return to the office, where I would stay till around 6 p.m. before going back out at around 10 p.m. to one of the exclusive nightclubs in Chelsea, where I would be looking for Prince Harry or Chelsea footballers. My shift would usually end at about 3 or 4 a.m., and would start all over again a few hours later. We worked a Tuesday to Saturday week, as it was a Sunday newspaper, but I cannot ever remember having two consecutive days off, as inevitably something happened that I needed to attend and report on. I was never allowed to switch off. Sometimes I lay awake at night, thinking about the things I was being asked to do, or reliving the testimonies I had heard in court that day from a paedophile's trial. Yes, teaching can be all-consuming and occupy your thoughts, but there are many jobs that use just as much mental energy.

I was asked to do some hideous things as a tabloid newspaper journalist – some bordering on the illegal – in the pursuit of a story. Morals were a hindrance. If you had any qualms about doing the things that you were asked to do, there was a constant reminder that there were hundreds of keen, eager people who wanted your job and that you could just step aside if you wouldn't do what was needed. Imagine my joy, then, in becoming a teacher and getting to use my strong moral purpose for good, changing lives and really making a difference to kids every day. Thirteen years later and I have had moments where I have been close to quitting, but the thing that always makes me stay is a reminder that no job is perfect and that it only takes one appreciative comment from a student or a kind gesture at work and I remember why I do what I do.

Voices from the profession

Penny Rabiger, Director of Engagement at Lyfta and former teacher

I was a teacher for ten happy years, until a change of circumstances meant that teaching wouldn't be an option for me anymore. Since then, I have had a fabulous time working in a number of incredible education organisations on their start-up to grown-up journey. A few years ago, after many ad hoc requests from teachers asking me to explain how I made the leap from teaching, I started the Sunday #Edujobs bulletin on Twitter. Every Sunday morning, I tweet links to ads for jobs like mine – jobs with strong moral purpose but that are not in the classroom.

But I do miss so much about teaching. I miss those intense relationships across the school community with children, parents, and other teachers and staff that dedicate their time and energy for the good of the next generation. I miss the shape of the school year, and even that feeling of emptiness on the last day of the academic year and the sleepless night every year before school starts again for another roller-coaster ride. But I don't miss the feeling of being 'always on', and I don't think I could thrive in the condensed, top-down, high-stakes, high-accountability 'madhouse' that teaching has become in this country.

Teachers that ask me to coach them into their next role, looking for something in the charity or social enterprise sector, are frequently shocked at the apparent drop in salary when looking at roles they might potentially apply for; this often makes them balk and stay in teaching, despite feeling burnt out and lacking in enthusiasm. But really, the per hour salary is probably the same, and in exchange you get your evenings, weekends and lunch breaks back. You can go to the toilet whenever you like, and no one will ever pop over to your desk and ask to observe you working, or micro-manage and scrutinise you in the way teachers often see as normal.

I have worked with ex-teachers who cannot get used to the thought of only 25 days of holidays a year, which is standard for most jobs. The thought of long stints of working without a week off every six weeks and no automatic two weeks at Christmas, two weeks at Easter and six weeks over the summer often leave them puzzled over how to sustain their energy and arrange childcare for their families. The very thought of working from home, being given trust and autonomy and having to arrange their workload around a set of rhythms and cycles not dictated from outside can leave ex-teachers having to overcome school-life Stockholm syndrome and submitting to being resocialised into a different kind of working world. The pace, the culture, the type of work and the intensity – one aspect trades off for another. The bottom line is that the grass isn't greener on either side; it's just a different landscape altogether.

Joanne Crossley, teacher of English

When I finished university, I was desperate to be a teacher. My mum, a primary head, was desperate to put me off. She thought I should aim for something 'better', since I had just graduated from Oxford. This is one of the aspects of class that is sometimes overlooked – as one of the first pupils at my school to go to uni, never mind Oxford, I seemed to carry the weight of a whole town's expectations of 'getting out of here'. Anyway, I decided to go to the Bar. I had graduated in English, but it was relatively easy to undertake a law conversion course before applying to Bar School. It was important to me to feel a sense of contributing something worthwhile and I felt that a legal aid practice would be similar to teaching in terms of public service.

I started off doing a range of work: criminal and civil trials, family cases, housing, etc. Gradually, I specialised in family law, doing mostly childcare work. Being involved in care proceedings, usually representing parents, is tough. The more senior you become, the more difficult the cases become. I have seen, at close quarters, every imaginable type of abuse and neglect. I have represented paedophiles, child killers, sadistic abusers, rapists and, of course, the victims of all of these crimes. The pressure is enormous. Cross-examining a professor of paediatric neurosurgery regarding the likely mechanism of head injuries that caused a child's death, often at a moment's notice, is very stressful. Over a career, this inevitably takes an emotional toll.

I have done many different jobs to support myself through years of study, and what I have learned is this: usually the choice is between stressful or boring. And boring brings its own problems, especially if it is a low-paid job. The job may not be stressful, but making ends meet is. I don't understand why so many teachers find it hard to acknowledge that other jobs can be stressful, time-consuming and thankless. Any job that requires a degree will require you to work some evenings and weekends. These jobs will also require you to be available to clients at unsociable hours.

In many other professions, you are expected to hustle and tout for work: bringing in clients is a big performance indicator. The idea that only teachers are observed or held accountable is also laughable. I was observed and my performance rated every single day in court. Most workplaces have performance measures; some (for example in a solicitors' firm) will be very intrusive and involve logging productivity throughout the day. The lack of any commercial imperative in the classroom is something many teachers will be unaware of, but for me, this is the single biggest difference in my two careers. As a barrister, I was self-employed, which brings a good deal of financial insecurity: no maternity pay, no sickness pay and no pay whilst we are in 'lockdown'. Some well-publicised barristers earn huge amounts, but most legal aid lawyers earn at a level comparable to SLT level.

At least now when I am working late into the night, I am pouring over *Macbeth* or *The Great Gatsby*, not a list of horrific fatal injuries or trawling through personal bank accounts looking for the missing millions. Also, however hard it gets, I know I will have a break of sorts every six or seven weeks. Two of my daughters want to become teachers and I will be recommending it wholeheartedly. If only to spite my Mum…

Anonymous, resident graduate assistant

I left teaching after teaching English for three years, because I wanted a break from what had become quite negative working conditions and a culture of stress. I went into a boarding role at a school on a one-year contract. There were many reasons for this, but the overriding one was the desire to experience a different sort of role that would leave me feeling 'positive' about working in a school again. This is definitely something that my new role enabled me to do, and I am incredibly grateful for this. However, I can't help but feel excited to go back into teaching at a new school in September.

Teaching can be difficult; that feels like a massive understatement at times. I have had my fair share of stress with marking assessments, attending meetings, preparing for parents' evenings, filling in reports and other admin tasks. One thing that you do get in teaching, though, is a sense of achievement. I have missed sharing my knowledge of my subject with students, especially when they are so keen and enthusiastic, as they often are at GCSE and A level. I have missed the humour of teaching. I fondly recall the in-jokes and the hilarious moments that you didn't see coming. I have missed the school trips and assisting with the school production. I have also missed the camaraderie of it all and the feeling of being part of something. Being a teacher in a school enables you to make brilliant friends with those with whom you have a shared experience and culture. I don't think this is something that I have seen to the same extent in any of my other roles.

I spend a lot of my time reading the tweets of educators and feeling a desire to be part of the 'world' of education in that way again. I certainly miss the routine of teaching and the predictability of how the term would progress, whilst also knowing that I should expect anything at any time. I wholeheartedly miss being able to help students on a personal, pastoral level, and I know that those I have helped have improved upon their academic performance too because of the work that I did and the support that I gave.

Teaching also provides you with opportunities for personal progression; I will be going back into teaching as a key stage coordinator and I have my sights set on positions of responsibility above that in the future. It also provides access to CPD, whether it is something the school runs or something you decide to do for yourself, such as a master's degree in education, as I have previously done. Being able to study and continue learning to benefit others as well as yourself is something that I don't think other careers place such a focus on.

Ultimately, I am acutely aware of the difficulties that teachers can face, but I cannot imagine wanting to do anything else. Teachers in schools show solidarity like nobody else and, if I can teach, I know that in the future, I will.

Lou Enstone, teacher of English

When I graduated from university with my degree in creative writing and English literature, it never occurred to me to consider teaching. I was young and newly married to a still-student guy, and so I needed to find a job quickly. I took one as a receptionist at an IT firm and then the tech bubble burst and I was made redundant at the tender age of 22. Luck led me to a secretarial job at one of the 'Big 5' accounting firms, and for the next 11 years that was what I did.

I found my skill set – namely managing really difficult senior partners – and became a project manager with some of the most volatile staff and clients. It was challenging work. I was on shift pretty much 24 hours a day and there were days when I was needed for overseas calls at 2 a.m. and 11 p.m. I arrived at the office at 7 a.m. and often didn't leave until 9 p.m. With three children under five at home, this was really difficult. My main problem was that I was placed in the firing line – often with only my wits to back me up – any time things went wrong. By 2008, I was speaking to some of the most well-paid business people in the world on a daily basis, taking calls from government and yet still scooting down to Fortnum's to buy someone's favourite jam. While I was offered the opportunity to complete the professional accounting exams, this held zero interest for me. My skills were as a communicator and a consummate organiser, and I had a memory like a computer. So I began to stagnate. I had nowhere to go. I was already in the most senior role available for my job type and I was being paid considerably more (at the tender age of 30) than any of my friends. But I was never at home. I worked in the evenings (if I got home) and at the weekends. Occasionally, I just stayed all through the night. I kept clean clothes at the office and used the in-house shower facilities. I loved my job and I hated it.

As time went on, the balance wasn't quite as equal as it was before. Then came the 2008 financial crisis, and without going into too much detail, there was a complete roller coaster that included a Treasury Select Committee hearing. I knew our industry would never be the same again, but I did want to stick around and see what happened. So, over a glass of champagne one evening, I told my boss I was thinking about becoming a teacher.

Here I am over ten years later, and I am so thankful for that decision. I work fewer hours, have less stress, more laughs, more variety...but less money! I couldn't be happier with the way things turned out.

What can I do?

If you are determined to leave the teaching profession, just taking a look at what other jobs outside of teaching are paying may be enough to put you off! Some people don't like the idea of starting at the bottom of the pile all over again or having to complete more training in another career, especially if this also has financial implications and means a period of no earning while the training is undertaken. It may be useful to speak to others who have left education and get them to chat honestly about the positives and negatives of their new jobs.

As outlined above by people who have left the profession, there are many positives to seeking employment outside of education or the traditional school environment. The most often cited seems to be the better work–life balance and lack of scrutiny that other careers seem to be blessed with, but this is certainly not true of many other professions. From the research interviews I held with teachers, it's not the teaching that seems to be the significant driver when people start to look at leaving teaching but the sheer volume of work that needs to be crammed into the working day and the expectation that it will be done at weekends or in the evenings if it is not completed at school. For years, education has been powered by the goodwill of teachers, but the fuel is now running low. There are also many other jobs that require work to be done in the evenings and weekends, and they don't get the buy-out of the holidays that teachers get. My husband is not a teacher and we have spent many an evening sitting at our laptops, completing work that we didn't have time for during the day. He also earns a lot less than me. Nobody is disputing that teachers work hard. We do. But we also reap fantastic rewards that I have never come across in any other career.

Yet for every teacher who dreams of leaving, hundreds more stay. They may have their bad days and wonder what on earth they're doing, but ultimately, the difference they are making and the many highs outweigh the lows. Much research has focused on why people choose to leave, but there is little on why people choose to stay. So, I asked the Education Twitter community for their reasons and the answers were interesting, relatable and touching. A sample of these are printed below. I hope they'll help you to reignite that fire for teaching and remind you that despite its many challenges, it really is the greatest job in the world.

Belinda Faulkner @BelindaTeaches · 6h
Replying to @HughesHaili
I love it. I love the kids & I love hearing my students want to be scientists because of me

Dr. Derrick Venning @Derrick_Venning · Apr 19
Replying to @HughesHaili
Ultimately because I wouldn't want students to receive the education I received. Working with young people also fills me with hope on a daily basis.

Aisha Thomas @thomas_aisha · Apr 19
Replying to @HughesHaili
This is more than professional. It is personal. My children are living and breathing the system. I need to be the change I want them to see.
#RepresentationMatters

Hugh OGILVIE @Hugsutd01 · Apr 19
Replying to @HughesHaili
I have finally found my true vocation. Nothing is perfect but it satisfies me intellectually and the insights from and positive relationships with students keep the fire ablaze.

Preserving Positivity

Laura Reader @laura_reader · Apr 19
Replying to @HughesHaili
I love working with children and making a difference, and I know this is where my abilities lie - I can do something to help and have a positive impact. I also invest in the next generation of teachers and enjoy nurturing talent in other staff.

♡   ⟲   ♥ 8   ↥

Sarah Wilson @SarahWilsonBFC · Apr 19
Replying to @HughesHaili
I enjoy being with a classful of children, no two days are the same. The children I've taught have made me laugh (and cry).
Also the holidays are good and so is the pay, at the moment (pre lockdown related stuff) my work life balance is good.

♡   ⟲   ♥ 6   ↥

David and Lee @thought_weavers · 10h
Replying to @HughesHaili
I want to be a role model for others -children and adults. A teacher is exactly that, someone who inspires a love of life and learning. That's my aim. If I get anywhere close to that I'll be making a difference.

♡   ⟲   ♥ 1   ↥

Moominmai @LittleMy2020 · Apr 19
Replying to @HughesHaili
The job, for all its frustrations, feels meaningful. Witnessing children make progress, socially, emotionally, academically is incredibly fulfilling.

♡ 1   ⟲   ♥ 3   ↥

Moominmai @LittleMy2020 · Apr 19
And children are great company.

♡   ⟲   ♥ 1   ↥

Dena Eden @MissEdenEnglish · 6h
Replying to @HughesHaili
Because the absolute worst day of teaching can always be transformed by one kid or one line in a book you're marking. The highs are just so much bigger than the lows.

♡   ⟲   ♥ 1   ↥

MrsHEnglish @MrsH_edu · Apr 19
Replying to @HughesHaili
I stay for those moments... The moment a child smiles because they "got it", the moment I mark a book and they went up a band and the moment a less confident student answers a question in class.

♡   ⟲   ♥ 9   ↥

Felicity Colville @TheRealMissRead · Apr 19
Replying to @HughesHaili
Love kids. Love teachers. Love history. Absolutely cracking hat trick - would pay to go back right now if it were safe to

♡   ⟲   ♥ 4   ↥

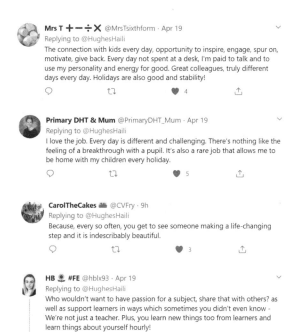

Mrs T ✚━➗✖ @MrsTsixthform · Apr 19
Replying to @HughesHaili
The connection with kids every day, opportunity to inspire, engage, spur on, motivate, give back. Every day not spent at a desk, I'm paid to talk and to use my personality and energy for good. Great colleagues, truly different days every day. Holidays are also good and stability!

♡   ↻   ♥ 4   ↥

Primary DHT & Mum @PrimaryDHT_Mum · Apr 19
Replying to @HughesHaili
I love the job. Every day is different and challenging. There's nothing like the feeling of a breakthrough with a pupil. It's also a rare job that allows me to be home with my children every holiday.

♡   ↻   ♥ 5   ↥

CarolTheCakes 🎂 @CVFry · 9h
Replying to @HughesHaili
Because, every so often, you get to see someone making a life-changing step and it is indescribably beautiful.

♡   ↻   ♥ 3   ↥

HB 🏆 **#FE** @hblx93 · Apr 19
Replying to @HughesHaili
Who wouldn't want to have passion for a subject, share that with others? as well as support learners in ways which sometimes you didn't even know - We're not just a teacher. Plus, you learn new things too from learners and learn things about yourself hourly!

♡ 2   ↻   ♥ 7   ↥

Conclusion:
Reason to stay
A call to arms

If you picked up this book with a totally negative mindset, determined to leave and knowing nothing would change your mind, chances are that you still feel the same. But if you love the job and were beginning to feel the frustrations and wondering if you should take the plunge, I hope this book has made you realise that you are not alone and that you will reconsider. Thousands of teachers up and down the UK have felt the same frustrations and almost buckled under the pressure placed upon them. However, they persevered and found ways around the challenges that teachers face, just as I have over my almost 15-year career. I hope both my story and their wisdom have given you some time to reflect, and that you feel able to go back into your classroom with a renewed freshness, vigour and determination. The strategies detailed are not groundbreaking, but they are tried and tested, and sometimes, when you are in a negative mindset, even the most obvious solutions become blurred in the muddied waters of dissatisfaction.

Now more than ever, you are needed. With teacher recruitment still failing to hit targets and students returning from an extended hiatus from school after COVID-19, we need to be there as a steady and sure presence to guide them through a world that may never be the same again. The public's perception of teachers is changing, and as parents struggle to homeschool their children, they are finally realising what those in the know have been aware of for decades: teachers are amazing! Experienced teachers have the wisdom of seeing many years of pedagogical change. They understand how students really learn. You are so vital to the students whose lives you enrich.

Over the years, like many of you, I have received numerous beautiful cards from year 11 students, filled with heartfelt messages. Perhaps one that will always stick out in my mind, which was sent to me six years after the girl left school, is this:

> When I was in year 11 and I wanted to write a story from the perspective of a hamster for my coursework and everyone was telling me that it was ridiculous because it was GCSE work but you LOVED it and encouraged me to do something out of the ordinary and I got an A ♥.

> Your mum spent absolutely ages turning up my prom dress for me because my grandma couldn't do it. Name one other teacher who goes that far for a student?

> When I had my baby, Violet, you sent a gorgeous package in the post when I haven't even seen you for four years... because you care so much about people. It's why I've always, ALWAYS looked up to you.

I don't print this to brag, or for validation that I am a great teacher. I am sure that you have all received similar messages and cards from kids whose lives you have enriched. I print it to remind myself and you that we make a difference. I hope you continue to do so for years to come.

References

Adopt a Classroom (2019) '4 Classroom Consumables Teachers Purchase'. Available online at: https://www.adoptaclassroom.org/2019/09/25/5-classroom-consumables-teachers-purchase-classroomconsumables/.

Allen, A., Benhenda, A., Jerrim, J. & Sims, S. (2019) 'New evidence on teachers' working hours. An empirical analysis of four datasets'. Available online at: https://johnjerrim.files.wordpress.com/2019/09/working_paper_teacher_hours.pdf.

Almer, E. D. & Kaplan, S. E. (2002) 'The effects of flexible work arrangements on stressors, burnout, and behavioral job outcomes in public accounting', *Behavioral Research in Accounting*, 14(1), pp. 1–34.

Baltes, B. B., Briggs, T. E., Huff, J. W., Wright, J. A. & Neuman, G. A. (1999) 'Flexible and compressed workweek schedules: A meta-analysis of their effects on work-related criteria', *Journal of Applied Psychology*, 84(4), pp. 496–514.

Bamford, S. & Worth, J. (2017) 'Teacher retention and turnover research: Research update 3: Is the grass greener beyond teaching?' Available online at: https://www.nfer.ac.uk/teacher-retention-and-turnover-research-research-update-3-is-the-grass-greener-beyond-teaching/.

Bandura, A. (1982) 'Self-efficacy mechanism in human agency', *American Psychologist*, 37(2), pp. 122–147.

Barsh, J., Cranston, S. & Lewis, G. (2009) *How Remarkable Women Lead: The breakthrough model for work and life*. London: Currency.

BBC (2012) 'Do you need to do two jobs?' Available online at: http://news.bbc.co.uk/1/hi/talking_point/1977131.stm.

BBC (2019) 'Teachers "paying for resources out of own money"'. Available online at: https://www.bbc.co.uk/news/education-47964154.

Bennett, T. (2017) 'Creating a Culture: How school leaders can optimise behaviour'. Available online at: https://assets.publishing.service.gov.uk/government/uploads/system/uploads/attachment_data/file/602487/Tom_Bennett_Independent_Review_of_Behaviour_in_Schools.pdf.

Bloom, N., Liang, J., Roberts, J. & Ying, Z. J. (2015) 'Does working from home work? Evidence from a Chinese experiment', *Quarterly Journal of Economics*, 130(1), pp. 165–218.

Bubb, S. & Earley, P. (2004) *Managing Teacher Workload: Work–life balance and wellbeing*. Thousand Oaks, CA: Sage Publications.

Cooper, H. & Mackenzie Davey, K. (2011) 'Teaching for Life? Midlife narratives from female classroom teachers who have considered leaving the profession', *British Journal of Guidance and Counselling*, 39(1), pp. 83–102.

Covey, S. R. (1989) *The 7 Habits of Highly Effective People: Powerful Lessons in Personal Change*. Utah: Franklin Covey.

Daily Mail, the (2012) 'Six blows on the rump! Extraordinary records reveal how corporal punishment was meted out in our schools'. Available online at: https://www.dailymail.co.uk/news/article-2122724/Records-reveal-corporal-punishment-dished-schools-1970s-Found-cellar-Greenfield-Primary-School-Oldham-Greater-Manchester.html.

Daily Mirror, the (2019) 'Worst schools staffing crisis in decades as new teachers quit in record numbers'. Available online at: https://www.mirror.co.uk/news/uk-news/worst-schools-staffing-crisis-decades-18890123.

Deci, E. L. & Ryan, R. M. (1985) *Intrinsic motivation and self-determination in human behavior*. New York, NY: Plenum.

Deci, E. L., Ryan, R. M. (2000) 'Self-determination theory and the facilitation of intrinsic motivation, social development, and well-being', *American Psychologist*, 55(1), pp. 68–78.

Department for Education (2014) 'Government evidence to the STRB: The 2015 pay award'. Available online at: https://assets.publishing.service.gov.uk/government/uploads/system/uploads/attachment_data/file/370590/141027_DfE_Evidence_to_STRB.pdf.

Department for Education (2016) 'Eliminating unnecessary workload around marking: Report of the Independent Teacher Workload Review Group'. Available online at: https://www.gov.uk/government/publications/reducing-teacher-workload-marking-policy-review-group-report.

Department for Education (2018) 'Factors affecting teacher retention: qualitative investigation research report'. Available online at: https://www.gov.uk/government/publications/factors-affecting-teacher-retention-qualitative-investigation.

Department for Education (2019a) 'Exploring flexible working practice in schools'. Available online at: https://www.gov.uk/government/publications/exploring-flexible-working-practice-in-schools.

Department for Education (2019b) 'Permanent and fixed period exclusions in England: 2017 to 2018'. Available online at: https://assets.publishing.service.gov.uk/government/uploads/system/uploads/attachment_data/file/820773/Permanent_and_fixed_period_exclusions_2017_to_2018_-_main_text.pdf.

Department for Education (2019c) 'Teacher workload survey 2019: Research report'. Available online at: https://www.gov.uk/government/publications/teacher-workload-survey-2019.

Department for Education (2020) 'Return to teaching'. Available online at: https://getintoteaching.education.gov.uk/explore-my-options/return-to-teaching.

Dolton, P., Marcenaro-Gutierrez, O. D., Pistaferri, L. & Algan, Y. (2011) 'If you pay peanuts do you get monkeys? A cross-country analysis of teacher pay and pupil performance', *Economic Policy*, 26(65), pp. 7–55.

Dreikurs, R. (1958) 'The Cultural Implications of Reward and Punishment', *International Journal of Social Psychiatry*, 4(3), pp. 171–178.

Dreikurs, R. (1964) *Children: The Challenge*. New York, NY: Hawthorn Books.

Edexec (2020) 'ASCL comment on plans over cancelled exams'. Available online at: https://edexec.co.uk/ascl-comment-on-plans-over-cancelled-exams/.

Edison Learning (2017) 'Ofsted's latest guidance to inspectors about marking and feedback'. Available online at: http://edisonlearning.net/ofsteds-latest-guidance-inspectors-marking-feedback/.

Education Endowment Foundation (2016) 'A marked improvement? A review of the evidence on written marking'. Available online at: https://educationendowment foundation.org.uk/evidence-summaries/evidence-reviews/written-marking/.

Education Endowment Foundation (2018) 'Performance pay: Low impact for low cost, based on limited evidence'. Available online at: https://educationendowmentfoundation.org.uk/evidence-summaries/teaching-learning-toolkit/performance-pay/.

Education Endowment Foundation (2019) 'Improving Behaviour in Schools'. Available online at: https://educationendowmentfoundation.org.uk/tools/guidance-reports/improving-behaviour-in-schools/.

Education Policy Institute, the (2018) 'Analysis: Teacher labour market pressures'. Available online at: https://epi.org.uk/publications-and-research/the-teacher-labour-market/.

Education Policy Institute, the (2019) 'School revenue balances in England'. Available online at: https://epi.org.uk/wp-content/uploads/2019/01/School-Revenue-Balances-in-England_EPI.pdf.

Education Support (2018) 'Teacher Wellbeing Index 2018 highlights stress epidemic and rising mental health issues across the sector'. Available online at: https://www.educationsupport.org.uk/about-us/press-centre/teacher-wellbeing-index-2018-highlights-stress-epidemic-and-rising-mental.

Epitropoulos, A. (2019) '10 Signs of a Toxic School Culture', *ASCD Education Update*, 61(9), pp. 10–14.

FairFX (2017) 'Avoid paying over the odds for your holiday'. Available online at: https://blog.fairfx.com/smart-money/avoid-paying-over-odds-your-holiday/.

Family and Childcare Trust (2018) 'Holiday Childcare Survey 2018'. Available online at: https://www.familyandchildcaretrust.org/holiday-childcare-survey-2018.

Gajendran, R. S. & Harrison, D. A. (2007) 'The good, the bad, and the unknown about telecommuting: Meta-analysis of psychological mediators and individual consequences', *Journal of Applied Psychology*, 92(6), pp. 1524–1541.

Glass, J. & Finley, A. (2002) 'Coverage and effectiveness of family responsive workplace policies', *Human Resource Management Review*, 12(3), pp. 313–337.

Greenberger, D. & Padesky, C. A. (2015) *Mind Over Mood: Change how you feel by changing the way you think.* New York, NY: Guildford Press.

Guardian, the (2012) 'Teachers tempted to rewrite pupils' exam answers'. Available online at: https://www.theguardian.com/education/2012/apr/02/teachers-under-pressure-to-cheat.

Guardian, the (2013) 'Secret Teacher: there is no autonomy in teaching today'. Available online at: https://www.theguardian.com/teacher-network/teacher-blog/2013/feb/16/secret-teacher-autonomy-teaching-trust.

Guardian, the (2018a) 'I know the real source of our classroom rot'. Available online at: https://www.theguardian.com/education/2018/apr/08/real-rot-in-uk-classrooms-problems-go-deeper-than-money.

Guardian, the (2018b) '"I will never return to teach in England": the UK teachers finding refuge abroad. An estimated 15,000 teachers are snapped up overseas each year, driven away by the stress in British schools'. Available online at: https://www.theguardian.com/education/2018/oct/02/never-return-teach-england-refuge-abroad.

Guardian, the (2018c) 'Ofsted inspectors to stop using exam results as key mark of success'. Available online at: https://www.theguardian.com/education/2018/oct/11/ofsted-to-ditch-using-exam-results-as-mark-of-success-amanda-spielman.

Guardian, the (2018d) 'Thousands of teachers caught cheating to improve exam results'. Available online at: https://www.theguardian.com/education/2018/feb/11/thousands-of-teachers-caught-cheating-to-boost-exam-results.

Guardian, the (2019) 'Fifth of teachers plan to leave profession within two years'. Available online at: https://www.theguardian.com/education/2019/apr/16/fifth-of-teachers-plan-to-leave-profession-within-two-years.

Hargreaves, A. & Shirley, D. (2012) *The Global Fourth Way: The quest for educational excellence.* Thousand Oaks, CA: Corwin.

Headspace (2020) 'A guided 10-minute meditation for calm and relaxation'. Available online at: https://www.headspace.com/meditation/10-minute-meditation.

Health and Safety Executive (2020) 'Work-related violence'. Available online at: https://www.hse.gov.uk/violence/.

Heus, P. D. & Diekstra, R. F. W. (1999) 'Do teachers burn out more easily? A comparison of teachers with other social professions on work stress and burnout symptoms'. In R. Vandenberghe & A. M. Huberman (eds), *Understanding and preventing teacher burnout: A sourcebook of international research and practice.* Cambridge: Cambridge University Press, pp. 269–284.

High Fliers (2020) 'The Graduate Market in 2020'. Available online at: https://www.highfliers.co.uk/download/2020/graduate_market/GM20Report.pdf.

Hodgson, J. & Greenwell, B. (2017) 'The Work of the Course: validity and reliability in assessing English Literature', *English in Education*, 51(1), pp. 100–111.

i newspaper (2019) 'These diaries show why teachers' workloads are driving so many to quit'. Available online at: https://inews.co.uk/news/education/diaries-show-why-teachers-workloads-drive-many-to-quit-501938.

Independent, the (2016) '"Dangerous and dilapidated" school buildings damaging to pupils' health and performance'. Available online at: https://www.independent.co.uk/news/education/education-news/dangerous-dilapidated-school-buildings-damaging-pupils-health-performance-a7025481.html.

Independent, the (2019a) 'Nearly one in four teachers physically attacked by pupils at least once a week, survey suggests'. Available online at: https://www.independent.co.uk/news/education/education-news/teachers-pupils-violence-classroom-behaviour-nasuwt-teaching-union-a8877776.html.

Independent, the (2019b) 'Teachers living in sheds, cars and using food banks as demand for grants rises, charity warns'. Available online at: https://www.independent.co.uk/news/education/education-news/teachers-food-banks-housing-shed-education-support-partnerships-schools-a9143366.html.

Judd, I. (2008) *Why Walk When You Can Fly: Soar beyond your fears and love yourself and others unconditionally*. Novato, CA: New World Library.

Kogon, K., Merrill, A. & Rinne, L. (2016) *The 5 Choices: The path to extraordinary productivity*. New York, NY: Simon & Schuster.

Labour Party (1997) 'Labour Party Manifesto'. Available online at: http://www.labourparty.org.uk/manifestos/1997/1997-labour-manifesto.shtml.

Leung, D. Y. P. & Lee, W. W. S. (2006) 'Predicting intention to quit among Chinese teachers: differential predictability of the component of burnout', *Anxiety, Stress, & Coping*, 19, pp. 129–141.

London News Online (2019) 'Teachers' union president reports on teaching staff using food banks due to low pay and high cost of living'. Available online at: https://londonnewsonline.co.uk/teachers-union-president-reports-on-teaching-staff-using-food-banks-due-to-low-pay-and-high-cost-of-living/.

Lynch, S., Worth, J., Bamford, S. & Wespieser, K. (2016) 'Engaging Teachers: NFER analysis of teacher retention'. Slough: NFER. Available online at: https://www.nfer.ac.uk/publications/LFSB01.

MaternityTeacher PaternityTeacher Project (2019) 'Links between gender and teacher retention'. Available online at: https://www.mtpt.org.uk/ (subscriber only).

McGrath-Champ, S., Wilson, R., Stacey, M. & Fitzgerald, S. (2018) 'Understanding work in schools: The foundation of teaching and learning'. Available online at: https://news.nswtf.org.au/application/files/7315/3110/0204/Understanding-Work-In-Schools.pdf.

McKinsey and Company (2007) 'How the world's best-performing school systems come out on top'. Available online at: https://www.mckinsey.com/industries/social-sector/our-insights/how-the-worlds-best-performing-school-systems-come-out-on-top.

Michel, A., Bosch, C. & Rexroth, M. (2014) 'Mindfulness as a cognitive–emotional segmentation strategy: An intervention promoting work–life balance', *Journal of Occupational and Organizational Psychology*, 87(4), pp. 733–753.

Michie, S. (2002) 'Causes and Management of Stress at Work', *Occupational Environmental Medicine*, 59, pp. 67–72.

Mirror, the (2019) 'More than 200 teachers died from asbestos – and kids are at risk in classroom'. Available online at: https://www.mirror.co.uk/news/uk-news/more-200-teachers-die-asbestos-15001788.

Money Saving Expert (2018) 'Teacher Tax Rebates'. Available online at: https://forums.moneysavingexpert.com/discussion/4367975/tax-rebate.

NASUWT (2017) 'The Big Question 2017: An opinion survey of teachers and school leaders'. Available online at: https://www.nasuwt.org.uk/uploads/assets/uploaded/7649b810-30c7-4e93-986b363487926b1d.pdf.

NASUWT (2020) 'Taking Control of your Performance Management'. Available online at: file:///C:/Users/haili/Downloads/Performance%20Management%20Teachers%20England.pdf.

National Education Union (2018) 'Securing pay progression'. Available online at: https://neu.org.uk/advice/securing-pay-progression.

National Education Union (2019) 'Violence in schools'. Available online at: https://neu.org.uk/advice/violence-schools.

NFER (2020) 'Teacher autonomy: how does it relate to job satisfaction and retention?' Available online at: https://www.nfer.ac.uk/teacher-autonomy-how-does-it-relate-to-job-satisfaction-and-retention/.

Office for National Statistics (2018) 'Labour Force Survey 2017–18'. Available online at: https://www.ons.gov.uk/releases/uklabourmarketstatisticsmar2018.

Ofsted (2019) 'Teacher well-being at work in schools and further education providers'. Available online at: https://assets.publishing.service.gov.uk/government/uploads/system/uploads/attachment_data/file/819314/Teacher_well-being_report_110719F.pdf.

Pearson (2017) 'Testing the Water'. Available online at: https://www.pearson.com/content/dam/one-dot-com/one-dot-com/uk/microsites/testing-the-water/documents/how-assessment-can-underpin-great-teaching.pdf.

Perry-Smith, J. E. & Blum, T. C. (2000) 'Work–family human resource bundles and perceived organizational performance', *Academy of Management Journal*, 43(6), pp. 1107–1117.

Policy Exchange (2016) 'The Importance of Teachers: A collection of essays on teacher recruitment and retention'. Available online at: https://policyexchange.org.uk/publication/the-importance-of-teachers-a-collection-of-essays-on-teacher-recruitment-and-retention/.

Policy Exchange (2018) '"It Just Grinds You Down": Persistent disruptive behaviour in schools and what can be done about it'. Available online at: https://policyexchange.org.uk/wp-content/uploads/2019/01/It-Just-Grinds-You-Down-Joanna-Williams-Policy-Exchange-December-2018.pdf.

Powell, S. & Tod, J. (2004) *A Systematic Review of How Learning Theories Explain Learning Behaviour in School Contexts*. London: EPPI-Centre, Social Science Research Unit, Institute of Education, University of London.

RIBA (2016) 'Better Spaces for Learning'. Available online at: https://www.architecture.com/knowledge-and-resources/resources-landing-page/better-spaces-for-learning.

Ro, E. (2018) 'Understanding reading motivation from EAP students' categorical work in a focus group', *TESOL Quarterly*, 52(4), pp. 772–797.

Schaufeli, W. & Enzmann, D. (1998) *The burnout companion to study and practice: A critical analysis*. London: Taylor & Francis Group.

Schools Week (2019) 'Assaults in schools soar by 72% in four years'. Available online at: https://schoolsweek.co.uk/assaults-in-schools-soar-by-72-in-four-years/.

Schools Week (2020) 'DfE's 2020 teacher pay proposals: Rise will cost schools £455m, plus 6 more findings'. Available online at: https://schoolsweek.co.uk/dfe-2020-teacher-pay-proposals-rise-will-cost-schools-455m-plus-6-more-findings/.

Shukry, M. (2017) 'Commodification of Education in United Kingdom', *Journal of Law and Society Management*, 4(1), pp. 38–47.

Sims, S. (2017) 'TALIS 2013: Working Conditions, Teacher Job Satisfaction and Retention'. Available online at: https://assets.publishing.service.gov.uk/government/uploads/system/uploads/attachment_data/file/656249/TALIS_2013_Evidence_on_Working_Conditions_Teacher_Job_Satisfaction_and_Retention_Nov_2017.pdf.

Skaalvik, E. M. & Skaalvik, S. (2011) 'Teacher job satisfaction and motivation to leave the teaching profession: Relations with school context, feeling of belonging, and emotional exhaustion', *Teaching and Teacher Education*, 27(6), pp. 1029–1038.

Slomp, D. H. (2008) 'Harming not helping: The impact of a Canadian standardized writing assessment on curriculum and pedagogy', *Assessing Writing*, 13(3), pp. 180–200.

Spain, S. M., Harms, P. D. & Wood, D. (2016) 'Stress, well-being, and the dark side of leadership', *Research in Occupational Stress and Well-being*, 14, pp. 33–59.

Teacher Tapp (2018) 'Emails take up almost a whole teaching day each week'. Available online at: https://teachertapp.co.uk/what-teachers-tapped-this-week-41-9th-july-2018/.

Telegraph, the (2019) 'Bad behaviour in classrooms fuelled by fashionable "restorative justice" schemes, teacher union chief says'. Available online at: https://www.telegraph.co.uk/education/2019/03/27/bad-behaviour-classrooms-fuelled-fashionable-restorative-justice/.

TES (2018) 'Exclusive: 70% of school buildings "not fit for purpose"'. Available online at: https://www.tes.com/news/exclusive-70-school-buildings-not-fit-purpose.

TES (2019a) '"As a teacher, it's impossible to plan a family holiday". In 13 years of teaching, this secondary teacher has managed just two family holidays abroad – and blames the profession for it'. Available online at: https://www.tes.com/news/teacher-its-impossible-plan-family-holiday.

TES (2019b) 'Quarter of teachers "may quit, mainly due to workload"'. Available online at: https://www.tes.com/news/quarter-teachers-may-quit-mainly-due-workload.

TES (2020a) 'Heads: Exam cancellation points to "less brutal" system: With teacher assessment being used to award grades this summer, heads hope that the exam system could be reviewed'. Available online at: https://www.tes.com/news/heads-exam-cancellation-points-less-brutal-system.

TES (2020b) 'How experienced teachers are losing out in pay deal.' Available online at: https://www.tes.com/news/how-experienced-teachers-are-losing-out-pay-deal.

Thomas, H., Butt, G., Fielding, A., Foster, J., Gunter, H., Lance, A., Pilkington, R., Potts, E., Powers, S., Rayner, S., Rutherford, D., Selwood, I. & Szwed, C. (2004) 'The Evaluation of the Transforming the School Workforce Pathfinder Project, Research Report 541'. (London, DfES) Available online at: www.dfespublications.gov.uk.

Times, The (2019) 'Parents asked to pay for teachers' salaries and school repairs'. Available online at: https://www.thetimes.co.uk/article/parents-asked-to-pay-for-teachers-salaries-and-school-repairs-x5mf0nhsj.

Tomsett, J. & Uttley, J. (2020) *Putting Staff First: A blueprint for revitalising our schools.* Woodbridge: John Catt Educational.

Williams, Y. & Williams, D. (2017) 'How accurate can A level English Literature marking be?', *English in Education*, 51(3), pp. 255–274.

Winn, G. L. & Dykes, A. C. (2019) 'Identifying Toxic Leadership & Building Worker Resilience', *Professional Safety*, 64(3), pp. 38–45.

YouGov (2018) 'Teachers: stressed and undervalued – but satisfied with their job'. Available online at: https://yougov.co.uk/topics/economy/articles-reports/2018/11/29/teachers-stressed-and-undervalued-satisfied-their-.

Your Money Sorted (2020) 'Is this why many teachers are leaving the profession?' Available online at: https://www.yourmoneysorted.co.uk/blog/teacher-leaving-profession.